Praise for Helen Ellis's

SOUTHERN LADY CODE

"It's hard to adequately describe these delightful autobiographical essays. Maybe that's because Alabama-born Ellis's take on Southern manners and mores is a unique blend of sardonic and sincere. More likely because it's difficult to formulate sentences when you're laughing this hard."   —*People*

"With a voice that's equal parts Nora Ephron and David Sedaris, this Alabama-raised, NYC-honed author should be your new woman crush."   —*Family Circle*

"Wry, candid, clever, and occasionally downright moving."   —Alabama Public Radio

"Helen Ellis returns with an essay collection about shifting moral codes as seen through the lens of her Southern upbringing. . . . Ellis's sense of humor and honesty never fail to charm."   —*The Wall Street Journal*

"Hilarious. . . . Devilish. . . . Grab a copy of the *Southern Lady Code* and let Helen Ellis whisper an outrageous story into your ear. She's a hoot-and-a-half (that's Southern Lady Code for funny as all heck). . . . Laugh-out-loud funny. . . . A literary cocktail of hilarious insights, snark, and shockingly good advice—best consumed with a vodka lemonade." —*Due South*

"Good advice and great reading. . . . Ellis kills."
—*St. Louis Post-Dispatch*

"Expecting out-of-town guests who need schooling in the ways of the South? Hand them a copy of *Southern Lady Code* by Helen Ellis." —*The Augusta Chronicle*

"A set of viciously funny essays that tackle marriage, thank-you notes and marijuana. You'll applaud the confidence she finds in donning a black-tie gown, and her paean to vacuuming will leave you in stitches. Ellis speaks her truth with a lipstick kiss." —*Observer*

Helen Ellis

SOUTHERN LADY CODE

Helen Ellis is the author of *American Housewife* and *Eating the Cheshire Cat*. Raised in Alabama, she lives with her husband in New York City.

SOUTHERN LADY CODE

SOUTHERN LADY CODE

· ESSAYS ·

Helen Ellis

ANCHOR BOOKS

A Division of Penguin Random House LLC

New York

FIRST ANCHOR BOOKS EDITION, APRIL 2020

Several pieces in this collection originally appeared in the following
publications: "Making a Marriage Magically Tidy" in the *New York
Times* column "Modern Love" (June 2, 2017); "How to Stay Happily
Married" in *Paper Darts* (Winter 2017); "Tonight We're Gonna Party
Like It's 1979" in *Eating Well* (November/December 2017); "How
to Be the Best Guest" as "An American's Guide to Being the Best
Guest" in *Financial Times* (March 2016); and "When to Write a
Thank-You Note" in *Garden & Gun* (February/March 2018).

The Library of Congress has cataloged
the Doubleday edition as follows:
Names: Ellis, Helen, author.
Title: Southern Lady Code : essays / Helen Ellis.
Description: First edition. | New York : Doubleday, 2019.
Identifiers: LCCN 2018019774
Subjects: LCSH: Women—Southern States—Conduct of life. |
Women—Southern States—Social life and customs. | Man-woman
relationships—Southern states. | Courtesy.
Classification: LCC PS3555.L5965 A6 2019 | DDC 814/.54—dc23
LC record available at https://lccn.loc.gov/2018019774

Anchor Books Trade Paperback ISBN: 978-0-525-56292-4
eBook ISBN: 978-0-385-54390-3

www.anchorbooks.com

Printed in the United States of America
10 9 8 7 6 5 4 3 2 1

for Elizabeth,

the best sister and my favorite reader

Southern Lady Code | *noun* | \ ˈsə-t<u>h</u>ərn ˈlā-dē ˈkōd \ :
a technique by which, if you don't have something nice
to say, you say something not so nice in a nice way

· CONTENTS ·

CONTENTS

SOUTHERN LADY CODE

MAKING

A MARRIAGE

MAGICALLY

TIDY

I have the reputation of living what Marie Kondo would call a "magically tidy" life. My tights are rolled like sushi, my tabletops are bare, my kitchen is so clean I could perform surgery in it. But I wasn't always this way. When I was twenty-three, I left my New York City apartment with a panty liner stuck to my back.

Yes, it was used. Yes, earlier that day, I'd taken it off and tossed it onto my twin bed like a bear throws salmon bones onto a rock. Once it was there, I guess I forgot about it. It was probably camouflaged. I promise you there was other stuff on the bed. My bed used to look like a landfill.

Maybe I threw my coat over it and it stuck. And then I put my coat back on and rode a bus thirty blocks with a panty liner between my shoulder blades. No, nobody said a word. I didn't know it was there until my date gave me a hug and then peeled it off like he was at a burlesque show in hell.

This was not the man I married.

The man I married walked into my apartment and found Pop-Tart crusts on my couch. I can still see his face, bewildered and big-eyed, pointing at the crusts as if to ask, "Do you see them too?"

I shrugged.

He sat on the sofa. It is my husband's nature to accept me the way that I am.

My nature is to leave every cabinet and drawer open like a burglar. My superpower is balancing the most stuff on a bathroom sink. If I had my druthers, I'd let cat puke dry on a carpet so it's easier to scrape up. If druthers were things, and I had a coupon for druthers, I'd stockpile them like Jell-O because you never know when you might need some druthers.

My husband fell in love with a creative woman. "Creative" is Southern Lady Code for *slob*.

But it is one thing to accept a slob for who she is; it is another to live with her.

A year into our marriage, my husband complained.

He said, "Would you mind keeping the dining room table clean? It's the first thing I see when I come home."

What I heard was: "I want a divorce."

What I said was: "Do you want a divorce?"

"No," he said. "I just want a clean table."

I called my mother.

Mama asked, "What's on the table?"

"Oh, everything. Whatever comes off my body when I come home. Shopping bags, food, coffee cups, mail. My coat."

"Your coat?"

"So I don't hang my coat in the closet—that makes me a terrible person? He knew who he was marrying. Why do I have to change?"

Mama said, "Helen Michelle, for heaven's sake, this is a problem that can be easily solved. Do you know what other married women deal with? Drunks, cheaters, poverty, men married to their Atari."

"Mama, there's no such thing as Atari anymore."

"Helen Michelle, some women would be beaten with a bag of oranges for sass talk like that. You married a saint. Clean the goddamned table."

And so, to save my marriage, I taught myself to clean.

Not knowing where to start, I knelt before the TV at the Church of Joan Crawford, who said as Mildred Pierce, "Never leave one room without something for another."

Yes, I'll admit she had a temper, but she knew how to clean.

You scrub a floor on your hands and knees. You shake a can of Comet like a piggy bank. You hang your clothes in your closet a finger's width apart. And no, you do not have wire hangers. Ever.

I have wooden hangers from the Container Store. They're walnut and cost $7.99 for a pack of six. I bought the hangers online because stepping into the Container Store for me is like stepping into a crack den. See, you're an addict trying to organize your crack, and they're selling you pretty boxes to put your crack in.

Pretty boxes *are* crack, so now you have more crack. But wooden hangers are okay. They're like mimosas. Nobody's going to OD on mimosas. Wooden hangers give you a boost of confidence. They make you feel rich and thin. They make a plain white shirt sexy. You promise yourself you'll fill one closet, and then you'll quit.

But I didn't quit. To keep my buzz going, I asked my husband if I could clean his closet.

He asked, "What does that mean?"

I said, "Switch out your plastic hangers for wooden ones. What do you think I mean?"

"I don't know, something new for Saturday night?" He did the air quotes: "Clean my closet."

My new ways were so new he assumed I was making sexual advances. It's understandable—so much dirty talk sounds so hygienic: salad spinning and putting a teabag on a saucer. It's like Martha Stewart wrote Urban Dictionary.

My husband opened his closet door and stepped aside. The man trusts me. I rehung his closet with military precision.

He said, "I never knew it could be this good."

We kissed.

And then I relapsed.

I don't know how it happened. Maybe it was leaving the Dutch oven to soak overnight. Maybe it was tee-peeing books on my desk like a bonfire. Maybe it was shucking my panties off like shoes. And then my coat fell off the dining room table. And I left it there because the cats were using it as a bed. There it stayed along with laundry, newspapers, restaurant leftovers (that never made it to the fridge), and Zappos returns.

My husband played hopscotch, never uttering a word of contempt, seemingly okay to coast on the memory of a pristine home as if it had been a once-in-a-lifetime bucket-list thrill like white-water rafting or winning a Pulitzer. Sure, he could have put things away, but every closet except for his was bulging and breathing like a porthole to another dimension.

I scared myself straight by binge-watching *Hoarders*. What do you mean, that lady couldn't claw her way through her grocery bag "collection" to give her husband CPR?

So I gave books I had read to libraries. Clothes I hadn't

worn in a year went to secondhand stores. I gave away the microwave because I can melt Velveeta on a stove.

And then came Marie Kondo's book *The Life-Changing Magic of Tidying Up*. Or as I like to call it: "Surprise, You're Still a Hoarder!"

Kondo's big question is: Does it spark joy?

I took a harder look around my home and answered: Pretty boxes of novel manuscripts that were never published did not spark joy. Designer shoes I bought at sample sales but never wore because they pinched my feet did not spark joy. My husband confessed that his inheritance of Greek doilies and paintings of fishing boats from his grandmother did not spark joy. So, out it all went.

And what is left is us. And my husband is happier. I'm happier, too. Turns out I like a tidy house. And I like cleaning.

Dusting is meditative. Boiling the fridge relieves PMS. Making the bed is my cardio, because to make a bed properly, you have to circle it like a shark. And all the while, I listen to audiobooks I would be too embarrassed to be caught reading. Not in the mood to clean a toilet? Listen to *Naked Came the Stranger,* and see if that doesn't pass the time.

The downside is that my husband has created a monster. I burn through paper towels like an arsonist. I joyride my vacuum—which has a headlight—in the dark.

And I don't do it in pearls and a crinoline skirt. It's not unusual for me to wear an apron over my pajamas.

I say, "Hey, it's me or the apartment. We can't both be pristine."

Without hesitation, my husband will always choose the apartment.

Sometimes, I invite him to join in my efforts, offering him the most awful tasks as if I'm giving him a treat. I'll say, "I'm going to *let you* scoop the cat box" or "I'm going to *let you* scrape the processed cheese out of the pan."

My husband says, "You're like a dominatrix Donna Reed."

I say, "Take off your shirt and scrape the pan, dear."

He takes off his shirt and scrapes the pan. In our more than twenty years together, my husband's nature hasn't changed.

Me, I'm a recovering slob. Every day I have to remind myself to put the moisturizer back in the medicine cabinet, the cereal back in the cupboard, and the trash out before the can overflows. I have to remind myself to hang my coat in the closet.

And when I accomplish all of this, I really do feel like a magician. Because now, when my husband comes home, the first thing he sees is me.

THE TOPEKA THREE-WAY

At a dinner party, the host fills a lull with: "Have I ever told you my Topeka Three-Way story?"

Now, this story does not take place in Topeka. I've changed the name of the city where it really takes place just like I'll change the names (and, while I'm at it, the personalities) of all of us who heard it. I'll call myself Bobbie Sue Gentry. That is the name of a lady who will give you the gory details. "Gory details" is Southern Lady Code for *flat Coke and faux pas*. If you repeat a word of it, Bobbie Sue Gentry will slit your tires.

I say, "You have not told us your Topeka Three-Way story."

By *us*, I mean me and my husband, Beauregard Beauregard Gentry. Yes, I like his made-up name so much, I've named him twice. Beauregard Beauregard is the name of a man who has biceps as big as beer cans and calls his wife "Mrs. Gentry" because he is so happily married to her. Mrs. Gentry (me with a 1970s Coppertone tan) calls her husband Beau Beau because honestly, who wouldn't?

Also present are another married couple: two male pickle-ball players who are not really pickle-ball players and not really gay men. But here's the thing: every party is made better by homosexuals; so, since it's my party, I'll add gay men if I want to.

Mr. Topeka says, "I was flying across the country to go to a wedding with Chichi in San Diego."

Chichi is the hostess and the storyteller's wife. In real life, she is the opposite of a Chichi. A Chichi nukes nachos and serves them to you while wearing an air-brushed halter top that reads CHICHI. The airbrushed *i*'s dot her nipples and her nachos are delicious, but Chichi is not Chichi and her husband is not Mr. Topeka. In real life, Mr. Topeka finds himself in dinner-party-worthy conversation situations because, as he puts it, he talks to everybody.

This stranger asked him to switch seats so that he could talk to the gorgeous young woman Mr. Topeka was sitting beside. I will not give this gorgeous young woman a new name, because gorgeous young women are never given names in such stories to begin with. They are called gorgeous young women, which I assume to most men means a rack like a loaf of Wonder Bread and an anime laugh.

Mr. Topeka says, "So, I look at this woman, and she

nods it's okay to switch seats. And I ask her, *Do you know this guy?* And do you know what she says?"

"It's her parole officer!" I say.

"What? No."

"You asked me to guess," I say. I am the kind of woman who considers every conversation a game show.

Mr. Topeka says, "No. She shakes her head, *No*. She doesn't know the guy. And he's wearing a wedding ring. And here's the kicker: SHE'S wearing a wedding ring, too!"

"Ooooo," says the dinner party, Chichi included.

A secret to a happy marriage is: be your partner's biggest fan. I wonder how many times Chichi has heard her husband tell "The Topeka Three-Way" and I wonder if she "Ooooo's" every time that she hears it. Every time Beau Beau hears me tell our "Cretan Gorge" story (which includes him force-feeding me protein bars, a donkey strike, and our leaving an elderly woman for dead), he drops his head to read his iPhone.

Mr. Topeka says, "So, we switch seats and the guy promises to buy me a drink, but he never does because we have to emergency land in Topeka."

"Ooooo," says the dinner party, Chichi included.

I ask, "Where's your new seat?"

A pickle-ball player asks, "What does it matter where he moved to?"

"Well, did the guy give up first class for this woman?"

Mr. Topeka says, "Back of the plane, right in front

of the toilet. Worst seat ever. But I could still see them canoodling."

Stop, you think, *no straight man says canoodling.* You think, *Can I trust my narrator?*

Well, of course you can't. Nobody retells a story word for word how they heard it. We embellish. We substitute. We censor. We lie. So, since I can't remember if Mr. Topeka's flight experienced turbulence or bad weather, let's just say: the wings were on fire, so they land.

Mr. Topeka says, "Everyone gets off the plane and gets vouchers for a hotel, and the guy says to me: 'I ordered a car, get in my car.' So, I get in his car and now there's four of us: me, the guy, the woman, and some new guy. And here's where Chichi gets mad at me."

Beau Beau says, "*Here's* where she gets mad at you?"

Chichi says, "For getting in a car with strangers."

Beau Beau says, "Mrs. Gentry would have been mad at me for switching seats on the plane."

"But then there'd be no story to tell."

"Mrs. Gentry would never let me tell this story to begin with."

It's true.

A secret to a happy marriage is: know your audience. Especially, your biggest fan. Beau Beau knows that I don't like to see movies in which a woman has natural childbirth; and he doesn't like to see devil possession. So we don't see these movies. And we don't tell stories the other one doesn't like to hear. For Beau Beau, I've stopped telling the "Bismarck Bear" story and the "Salem Horse" story because—even though these stories are hilarious—Beau Beau thinks, as he puts it, that he comes off like an idiot. I don't like to come off as anything other than the only woman in the world, so Beau Beau can't tell stories about his sex life before me. He can't tell stories about other women in general. I don't care if the story is about a pharmacist who sold him Odor-Eaters, I don't like stories where women get too close to my man.

Mr. Topeka says, "So, we get to the hotel and there aren't enough rooms, so I agree to room with the new guy, and the canoodlers get a room together. Then the four of us meet up in the hotel bar. And we're drinking and dancing, and I'm wasted. I mean, I've never been so drunk in my life. And then it's last call, and the three of them are heading off to the woman's room, and they ask me if I want to go with them."

"Ooooo," says the dinner party, Chichi included.

"But I go back to my room alone. I pass out. But then I wake up to my roommate looking through his bag for condoms because they've run out of condoms!"

"Ooooo," says the dinner party, Chichi included.

"And he tells me what's been going on with him and the other two. He names every position I've heard of, and then he asks me, 'Are you *sure* you don't want to join us?' And I tell him, 'Thanks, but no thanks.' "

"Wait," I say. "So you weren't in a three-way?"

Mr. Topeka says, "Nope. If I was, it would be called 'The Topeka FOUR-Way.'"

"Ahhh," says the dinner party, and Chichi claps her hands.

A secret to a happy marriage is: make yourself the good guy. Give your biggest fan a reason to applaud. Chichi is happy because her husband did not cheat on her. "The Topeka Three-Way" isn't a story about a three-way; it's a story about how Mr. Topeka is in love with his wife.

Now there is an expectation for the rest of us to outdo this story. The new story should be sexual, involve strangers, or be about a plane crash. The storyteller should be a more active participant. The storyteller should be prepared to pantomime a few things.

I look at Beau Beau and there is a telepathic back-and-forth of:

Don't tell your three-way story.

Don't tell YOUR three-way story.

Don't tell your story about pudding wrestling.

Don't tell YOUR story about stumbling into an adult film set.

So we don't say anything because sometimes the best stories don't need to be shared. I may not be a reliable narrator, but I am a reliable wife.

HOW TO STAY

HAPPILY MARRIED

On his birthday, give him a singing card and shave above your knees. On Halloween, cap your teeth with candy corn and leap out from behind the living room sofa. On Thanksgiving, dab a little Campbell's Cream of Mushroom soup behind each ear. On Super Bowl Sunday, incorporate a giant "#1" foam finger into your lovemaking.

Don't get angry with your husband when he sneezes too loud. Don't get angry when he sneezes more than three times in a row.

Don't tell your husband how he *almost* messed up.

Don't walk around with a bathrobe pocket full of Kleenex. Don't let your big beige panties hang over the lip of the hamper. Don't let him see you get out of an athletic bra or into a pair of control-top panty hose. Don't wear eyeglasses on a neck leash. Don't lotion your elbows in front of him in bed.

Don't remake the bed after your husband makes it. If your husband is loading the dishwasher, he's loading it "right."

Accept it: every time you cry out from another room, your husband isn't going to call out, "Are you okay?"

Quit quoting *When Harry Met Sally* and *Carrie* and *Fatal Attraction* and *9 to 5*. No matter how many times you say, "Oh, I've been looking for a red suede pump" or "They're all going to laugh at you!" or "I'm not going to be ignored, Dan!" or "I'm gonna change you from a rooster to a hen with one shot!" your husband will never get the references.

Nor will he understand why the *good* dermatologist and the *good* gynecologist cost so much.

If you can afford it, have separate bathrooms. If you can't, have separate peanut butter jars.

Buy earplugs and scented candles. Buy eye masks. Buy birthday gifts from the two of you. Write thank-you notes and forge his signature.

If you can't say anything nice, lock yourself in the bathroom. If you don't know how to say you're sorry, say it with fondue. If you're in the mood for love, stand in front of the TV naked. As long as your wedding ring fits, you haven't let yourself go.

FREE TO BE . . .

YOU AND ME

(AND CHILDFREE)

When I was nineteen, I sat my parents down and said, "I want to go on birth control and I want you to pay for it."

Papa looked at Mama. Mama looked like she'd stepped on a rake. Papa nodded. Without a word, they stood and walked out of my childhood home.

Mama always said, "Helen Michelle, you can tell us anything. We may not like it. We may walk away from you and walk around the block a few times to cool off, but we will always come back. And we will always help you."

Asking my parents to put me on the pill so I could have college sex with my never-went-to-college twenty-four-year-old boyfriend is the only time I've made my parents walk around the block.

Up until then, I'd been a good girl.

Growing up in Alabama, good girls kept to themselves and stayed out of trouble. Pregnancy was trouble. The risk of pregnancy was just as much trouble. A "pregnancy risk" is Southern Lady Code for *making out in your bathing suits*. In high school, I didn't know anyone on the pill. A Southern young lady's birth control was an aspirin pinched between her knees. Mama's departing words every time I left our Tuscaloosa house to go on a date or to a party were: *Jump up and down and be sweet! And don't let anybody touch your woo-woo!* The letter *A* was for Abstinence. You never said the other A word, but if you did it was a whisper.

Alabama was not—and I don't think *is*—an abortion-friendly state. Remember: Birmingham is where a man made the FBI's Ten Most Wanted list by bombing a Southside abortion clinic, killing a security guard. The bomber's brother was so upset by the manhunt that to protest, he cut off his own hand with a circular saw. And he videotaped it. And then he drove himself to a hospital. EMTs were sent to his house to collect the hand, and a surgeon reattached it. This is Southern Gothic country. Our zealots don't play.

I come from a very real place where girls missed seventh-grade roll call because "She havin' her baby!" High school girls really did have babies in my high school bathrooms. Ambulances never got there in time because full-term fetuses—fueled by Mountain Dew and Betty Crocker frosting straight out of the can—rocketed from fourteen-to-eighteen-year-old vaginas like a Six Flags log ride.

The alternative to showing up to school hugely pregnant was to disappear altogether. Some girls moved away to "spend time with their aunt" and then returned to school months later, deflated and forlorn. If they'd had the babies and given them to relatives to raise, or given them up for adoption, or *had it taken care of* somewhere up north, I do not know. Rumors spread that the girls had really been in insane asylums, and those rumors were not disputed. Better to be crazy than a slut.

Once a slut, a girl was forever after a slut. And getting pregnant was always blamed on the slut.

We did have Sex Ed, but you had to get a signed permission slip to attend the class, which—to avoid mixing church and state—was taught outside the school building in a double-wide trailer. Mama had had "the talk" with me and bought me several books about feminine hygiene and "becoming a woman," but I wrote this anonymous question for the teacher: "How do you pee with a tampon in?"

The answer was: "You hold the string."

I had no idea what this meant because I was so sexually inactive, I thought pee and menstrual blood came out of the same hole. It was also rumored that a tampon could pop your hymen and ruin your wedding night because your husband would want to divorce you when he found out he hadn't married a virgin.

I wasn't brave enough to use tampons until I was a high school junior. I was even less brave about walking over the train tracks to the Harco drugstore and buying them. I called Mama at her law office and asked her to "pick me up some supplies" on her way home. After a few minutes of back and forth, she figured out I didn't mean No. 2 pencils. She came home with a blue box in a brown paper bag. The Tampax how-to diagram of the female anatomy looked like the illustration of sink pipes on a bottle of Liquid-Plumr. I was supposed to raise a knee? It took me a few tries, but I figured it out.

When I decided to have sex as a college sophomore, I made sure it would be on my terms: I had to be in love, be in a committed relationship, and have rendered my reproductive system as infertile as a carburetor. Plus, I required a clean bill of health. As a result of coming of age in the eighties, every man I've chosen to have sex with, including my husband, had to take an AIDS test and have his doctor fax me his negative results. And use a condom.

To get a prescription for the pill, Mama made an appointment for me to have my first gynecologist appointment with her OB/GYN. But it was my grand-mother, my father's mother, who drove me to the doctor's office.

Grandmother sat in the waiting room, wearing white gloves and holding her Kelly bag on top of her lap the same way she used to sit on a bench and wait for me to come out of the snake house at the Birmingham Zoo. The ultimate example of a Southern lady, Grandmother—prim and proper with a perm-and-set—stood by in support of all of my alternative choices.

When I came out of the exam room I was crying. The doctor had put his hands on me in an unprofessional way and lectured me about the sin of premarital sex. He'd said, "I'd never let my daughter go on the pill."

Grandmother got the prescription from the doctor and took me to the pharmacy. Mama got a new gynecologist. I found out that sex was for good girls, but heartbreak was bad. I was devastated when my boyfriend left me a year later, but I kept taking the pill.

I stayed on the pill for no zits and big tits.

I married for love.

I went off the pill because I considered getting pregnant.

I was in my early thirties, and my husband and I had been married for years. There'd been a lot of reasons—nothing you haven't heard before—for why we had been "waiting to try." "Trying" is Southern Lady Code for *telling everyone and your mother that you're having intercourse to conceive.* "Waiting" is actively not doing what other people are waiting for you to do.

I heard: *When are you going to have kids? How many kids are you going to have? You're so good with kids. You should have kids; you'd make such a great mom.*

But I was scared of pregnancy. A friend of mine got gestational diabetes. A friend of a friend developed some sort of temporary paralysis. Another friend got a dark line over her lip that looked like Steve Harvey's moustache. Not to mention puking and walking around with a human being treading your uterus like a gerbil ball.

I was also scared of giving birth. I am the kind of woman who gets frustrated when crushed ice gets stuck in my straw. A friend of mine broke her tailbone pushing. A friend's friend separated her pelvis. There's something called "the ring of fire" that ain't a Johnny Cash song. And, once the baby's out, your vagina looks like—as one friend's husband so eloquently described it—"A raw steak torn in half."

But most of all, I was scared of cesareans. The cesarean rate on the Upper East Side is like one in three. It's easier to get your stomach sliced in half than get a prescription for Sudafed. And the baby's not pulled out like Baby Jessica from that well. Your doctor takes out your uterus and whatever else is attached, cuts out the baby, and then stuffs all your stuff back into your torso like she's on the run in a made-for-Lifetime movie and is packing an escape bag.

But some women love cesareans.

A friend said, "I carried twins for nine months, I wasn't going to *push*."

Me, I wasn't going to push my husband.

And by my mid-thirties, the way I understood how things worked in a marriage was that it was the wife's job to push to get pregnant.

I don't know any married woman who did not orchestrate her own pregnancy. Whether she went off birth control or was never on it to begin with, she had unprotected sex and she got pregnant. That's how you get pregnant. The only household accidents I believe in are Crock-Pot fires and tub slip-and-falls. I know women who poked pinholes in condom wrappers. I know women who got their husbands drunk, but not drunk enough to not get it up. Some women took their temperature to track ovulation. Some women bought apps for that. Sex was scheduled. Sex was abstained from and then scheduled.

I didn't do any of this. And by thirty-eight, I'd never been pregnant.

I heard: *You won't know what real love is until you have kids. Why get married if you're not going to have kids? Mar-*

ried women who don't have kids are selfish. Women who don't want to have their husband's babies don't really love their husbands. You don't WANT kids? Why don't you want kids? You don't LIKE kids? You think your cats are your kids?

My answer to all of this was: "If it happens, it happens."

My husband agreed.

My gynecologist said, "I can get you pregnant in your forties, but it's going to take a lot of work."

I did not want my gynecologist to get me pregnant. Or be pregnant in my forties. Or work at it.

Friends of mine were working on it and it looked like hard work. They got shots to increase their fertility. They got shots to maintain their pregnancy. They got IVF. They miscarried. They got IVF again. They froze their eggs. They hired surrogates. Their surrogates miscarried. Babies were born prematurely. Multiple babies were born. Some babies had "issues," which is Southern Lady Code for anything from a lazy eye to no eardrums. Postpartum was crippling. Marriages suffered.

I didn't want my marriage to suffer. We had it pretty great, my husband and I. No debt, little stress, we had our health, we loved each other. We worked well as a pair. And me, I didn't want to suffer either.

I am a woman who grew up during the seventies feminist movement. Marlo Thomas and friends gave me life anthems with the album *Free to Be . . . You and Me*. Rosey Grier told me it's all right to cry. Diana Ross told me when I grow up, I don't have to change at all. And Marlo assured me that "Mommies are people, people with children." But why did there have to be a song reminding folks who you are after you become a parent? That song had stuck with me. If I had children, would I cease to be me?

All my life, I'd thought of having kids with the seriousness that I'd thought of taking a ceramics class. When I finally took one and came home with three beautifully glazed but warped bowls, my husband said: "You're not going to turn into a lady who makes pots, are you?"

I was not. I kept the bowls and display them proudly—one holds fruit, one batteries, one loose change—but I had no interest in making anything else.

I called Mama and asked her if she'd be disappointed if I didn't have kids.

Mama said: "Helen Michelle, I didn't have children to have grandchildren."

And with that, I gave myself permission to let the idea of having kids go.

My husband and I had had fun playing with the idea. We'd picked out names: Kid and Mary Alice. Kid for a boy or a girl. Mary Alice for my husband's mother and grandmother. We'd thought about adoption and scrolled foster care sites, where kids' pictures are posted along with one-paragraph descriptions. You can sort them by age, sex, and race. You can refine your search by what *issues* you think you can handle. We'd felt a connection to a pair of siblings—a hyperactive six-year-old and a non-talkative four-year-old—named Star and Devlon. But we didn't reach out for them. And when I knew I was ovulating, we didn't have sex. And my husband never *pushed me*. Because it turns out, "If it happens, it happens" is Southern Lady Code for *we don't want kids*.

Not having children is one of the nicest surprises of our lives.

We do what we want, when we want. We do for each other. We do well for ourselves. We enjoy life's little pleasures. For my husband this means playing softball for six hours every Saturday and Sunday like he has since he was twenty-one. For me, it means sitting uninterrupted on my toilet every morning and working the *New York Times* crossword puzzle until I fill in every square or my legs go numb.

See, I always knew I wanted to fall in love and be married, I just wasn't sure if I wanted to have kids. Or maybe I was sure. Maybe I knew that we didn't need to start a family because the two of us are a family. And maybe I knew that I didn't need children, because I already have it all.

A ROOM

OF ONE'S OWN

(THAT'S FULL OF

GAY MEN)

W hen my friend Carmine asked if I'd like to be the sole lady at his bachelor party, my exact words were: "Sweet God in heaven above, yes."

I'd been waiting twenty years in Manhattan to receive an invitation like this. And, at forty-two, I'd finally gotten it. Carmine and his longtime beau, Bernard, were engaged and I couldn't wait to help celebrate. Some girls dream of moving to New York City to be a big star, but my dream was to be the only woman in a room of gay men.

Growing up in Alabama, there were no gay men.

In my high school graduating class of 1988, certain boys were "shy" or "respectful." "Artistic" or "sensitive." Some "kept to themselves." This was all Southern Lady Code for something, but at the time, we girls weren't exactly sure what. We thought of these boys like brothers. Or backup plans. I personally had secret alliances with a few. If we weren't married by the age of thirty, we'd marry each other. I married at thirty-one. All of my backup plans married women and had kids straight out of college.

Plan A had been to save myself for Michael Jackson, George Michael, or Boy George because these men were different. Two out of three had dated Brooke Shields, so they were obviously marriage material. Would I like to wake up every morning to the dulcet tones of an angel or shop for Day-Glo shorty-shorts? I most certainly would. Did I have a poster of Culture Club over my bed because I thought the lead singer with his Karma Chameleon braids was the man for me? I most certainly did. I copied his kabuki makeup. I thought, *When we go on our honeymoon, we'll share a Caboodle.*

The cliché Southern man is a gun-toting, tobacco-chewing redneck who rides a tractor like an inflatable pool toy and slurs racism like Carol Channing slurred her way through *Hello, Dolly!* But my favorite kind of Southern cliché is a fabric-book-carrying, mint-julep-sipping mama's boy who knows all the words to Julia Sugarbaker's "The Night the Lights Went Out in Georgia" rant and doesn't need to be asked to give you his opinion on anything. Especially Patsy Cline. Or personalized note cards.

Growing up, I did not think of this kind of man as homosexual, I thought of him as *Southern Effeminate*.

Southern Effeminate men are eccentric. They wear seersucker and bow ties. They garden and read and paint miniatures. They antique. They collect salt shakers and cookie jars, linens and art. They see their mothers every Sunday. They escort rich widows to cultural events. They help their women friends wax their legs and lip-sync "Love Is Strange" by Mickey and Sylvia in a talent show like Anthony Bouvier did on *Designing Women*.

Now, when I meet a man who carries a dog like a monocle and has an accent as peppery as white gravy, I think, *Is he gay or Southern Effeminate?*

Grandpapa was such a Southern man. He was funny. He buttered onions. He owned and played a piano. He dressed well. He had an umbrella stand of polished walking sticks. He let his daughter, my mama, raise forty-five cats in their backyard. When I earned top academic honors in college, he speed-needlepointed a ninety-inch rug runner to the soundtrack of *Oklahoma!* that read: "Lawdy! Lawdy!! My Gran'chile Is Summa Cum Laude!" When I slept on an egg-crate mattress pad on the floor of my first Manhattan apartment for eight months, he bought me a twin bed and box spring. Every year for my birthday, he sent me the amount of money of the age that I was. So, the year he gave me the bed, he also gave me twenty-two dollars.

Grandpapa and I got on fine because I wrote my thank-you notes. Not everyone wrote their thank-you notes, and if you didn't write your thank-you notes, he cut you off. My sister never got more than thirteen bucks. And to *really* teach her a lesson over the following years, Grandpapa sent her cash-enclosed birthday cards that were empty.

Grandpapa had a dark side. A *shady* side is more like it.

"Have a nice day, sir!" someone would say. And Grandpapa, with a singsong voice that sounded like *coochie coochie coochie coo,* would say, "I'll have any kind of goddamn day I goddamn want to!"

Grandpapa never ate at a restaurant without sending food back. He gossiped. He carried grudges like hand-kerchiefs. He dropped the N-word like marbles from a busted bag of marbles. And then there was the man who I'll call Norman.

After Grandpapa's wife—my grandmama—died when I was an infant, and then Grandpapa's next-door neighbor—his mama—died when I was a kid, and then two spinster sisters drove their car through the side of his house, he moved from Yazoo City, Mississippi, to Cincinnati and moved in with Norman.

As far back as I can remember, Norman was always in our Kodak pictures. He was younger than Grandpapa, closer to my parents' age, but I always thought of him and Grandpapa as a matching set. Grandpapa and Norman came to our school events and on vacations. Grandpapa and Norman traveled for free on cruise ships because they agreed to dance with all the single octogenarian ladies. Norman was never called *Uncle* Norman. He was just Norman. They were roommates. They were friends. They hosted family holidays. And when we stayed in their home, Grandpapa and Norman stayed at a hotel.

Grandpapa died when I was twenty-four. As Papa drove my sister, Mama, and me to the graveyard, Mama reviewed Grandpapa's eulogy—which he'd handwritten himself, underlining certain words for emphasis—but then stopped, looked up, turned to my father, and asked, "Mike, do you think Papa was gay?"

"Yes," he said.

And that is all I've ever heard spoken about it. It was also the last time we spoke to Norman, who immediately moved to Florida and moved in with another man.

So why did—and *do*—Southern men keep their homosexuality a secret?

I'm sure there are a lot of reasons. Religion is a big one. To a lot of us, the threat of eternal damnation is more real than ozone depletion. Jerry Lee Lewis could marry his thirteen-year-old first cousin once removed, but if he'd gone to bed with the "Chantilly lace and a pretty face" of another man, he'd have gone to hell. He might as well have started weaving a hand basket. But cane and wicker crafts could make you a target. When I was a teenager, certain Southern boys got jumped in parking lots.

And again, not because they were gay as in homosexual, but because they were Southern Effeminate: quiet or small or smart or they dared to wear something other than Wranglers. One pair of Howard Jones parachute pants and a rattail would get you a Pepsi can thrown at your head.

Some boys ducked and covered with us young ladies. Looking back, I was a member of what I'm now pretty sure were two tribes of Three Girls and a Gay.

In one group, the boy named each of us after one of Judy Garland's witches of Oz. There was the wicked one and the dead-to-the-world one. I, of course, was Glinda. To show me his devotion, this boy gave me an envelope filled with his fingernail clippings. Such flattery! I never felt so adored.

In the other group, the boy was our designated driver after each of us girls had chugged a Bartles & Jaymes Exotic Berry wine cooler. We thanked him for his support by letting him sleep on the floor during our slumber parties. At my house, boys weren't allowed in my bedroom, but Papa took one look at this kid and waved him out of the living room and on up the stairs. I'd thought it was because the boy was so homely that Papa didn't think he stood a chance with me. Now I know my father must have known what he knew about Grandpapa. But Papa, unless he was directly asked, was too considerate to let on.

Did I know these two boys were gay? Absolutely not. They never said they were, it never occurred to me to ask, and I honestly don't know if they are now because I don't do Facebook. But what I do know is that nobody bothered them in high school because they were shielded by us girls. And we girls could flirt and get tipsy without fear of having our reputations ruined. It was a wimp-wimp situation. We were all safe from regular boys.

At Central High, on the eve of the last day of tenth grade, a regular boy and his lackeys went after a Southern Effeminate boy because—as far as I can recall—he had a funny *name*. They rolled that boy's house with Quilted Northern, blacked out every window with split Oreos, salted obscenities in the grass, and shaving-creamed the cars. And the next day, they sold T-shirts commemorating the prank.

A local business had customized and printed those teal-and-white T-shirts without question. The regular boys sold them out of cardboard boxes in the school cafeteria. No teacher stopped them, and as far as I know, all 868 of us tenth graders bought one. Me included, I'm ashamed to admit. But so did the victim. That kid was so tough-skinned and ahead of his time, he considered himself a celebrity. Rightly so. Thirty years later, his name is one of the few I remember.

When I return to the South, I'm always unsettled when a man I assume is gay—because he has a face pulled tighter than a gift bow or starts every sentence with *"GIRL, please!"*—introduces me to his wife. Or when a straight man qualifies a comment that could be taken "the wrong way." For instance, on a Delta flight out of Atlanta, a good ole' boy in a trucker's cap that read AMERICAN BY BIRTH, BUT SOUTHERN BY THE GRACE OF GOD struck up a conversation with me by saying, "Now, I'm not gay or anything, but I like making jam!"

After twenty-five years in New York City, I still get a thrill when I meet a man who's out of the closet. Most gay men I meet here are out of the closet. So I live my life regularly delighted.

My friend Martin was my gateway gay. He's four years younger, so I didn't know him at Central High, but after I left for college, he took my sister to a dance. There is a photo of them standing shoulder to shoulder in our front yard. He was so "respectful" he never even tried to hold her hand. When Martin moved to Manhattan, we became friends. And like Heather Locklear in a Faberge Organics shampoo commercial, Martin introduced me to two of his gay men friends and they introduced me to two of theirs. Through Martin, I met Bernard; and through Bernard, I met Carmine.

In our thirties, Martin started a book club that was half gay men, half women. All the women, except for me, got pregnant and dropped out. When the last to leave—a woman who'd grown up in Manhattan—was debating whether to quit, she said to me, "I just don't want to spend two hours a month listening to a bunch of queens bitch about books."

I said, "That is *all* I want to do."

To me, a room full of gay men is like Narnia. It's a place I hoped was out there, on the other side of a closet door, full of talking lions that I always *deep down* suspected could talk.

To be beckoned into such a world makes me feel incredibly special.

Carmine's bachelor party was at Raoul's, an old haunt of an Italian restaurant on the Lower East Side. At the time, I had a Louise Brooks bob and still wore a Boy George red matte lip. I slipped into my highest heels and a chocolate-brown Tory Burch mini dress with white piping. The dress was stiff and had a deep V-neck. Nobody there would be interested in my cleavage, but I jockeyed up my breasts like I was setting out Waterford crystal ashtrays.

I made an effort.

I knew I was never going to be Cher or Barbra Streisand, but I could be Karen Walker or Auntie Mame: a fabulous lady of a mature age who can hold her liquor and carry on a conversation.

My friend Jason arrived and escorted me up a winding staircase to a private dining room. Hors d'oeuvres were passed by older professional male servers, the likes of which you'll find more commonly in the French Quarter. I was introduced to some kind of vodka that's not made from potatoes and thus doesn't get you fat. Guests mingled before a candlelit table for twelve. There were architects, doctors, and lawyers. Men in publishing and TV. All were at the top of their games. I was the housewife. But it was my place card set next to Carmine's.

At the far end of the room were a man and a woman whom nobody knew.

When the best man gave the first toast he ended it by saying, "Now, Carmine, to make sure you really want to marry Bernard, this heterosexual couple is going to have sex for us."

The collective gay gasp was strong enough to suck the tablecloth out from under the china.

"Just kidding!" said the best man.

Throughout supper, the man played a keyboard and the woman sang every Broadway show tune related to marriage. There are a lot of such songs. She sang through cocktail hour and two courses.

Dessert was brought out by two waiters, who weren't waiters. They were younger than our waiters. They were younger than all of us. They were gorgeous. They set down flourless cakes and, before anyone could take a bite, stripped nearly naked. There is a picture of me screaming with abandon with my hand on an ass cheek that is as chiseled and polished as Michelangelo's *David*. If Michelangelo was into Puerto Ricans.

What happened after that, I'll keep a secret. Because I want to continue to be invited into rooms of men with nothing to hide.

THE OTHER WOMAN'S

BURBERRY COAT

This isn't my trench coat, but it looks like my trench coat. It's Burberry and tan; but on the Upper East Side of Manhattan, women have tan Burberry trenches like women in the South have gigantic dogs. It's the same size as my coat and the lining is plaid like my coat, the pocket has a MetroCard in it like my coat did, but the belt buckle is wrong. My buckle was metal, it clanked when I walked. This buckle is plastic. Or leather. I can't tell the difference and I don't know which material signifies the more expensive coat—there must be a difference. This trench coat feels cheaper. Mine cost $795, which is more than my wedding dress (a charcoal-gray cocktail number I bought off the rack). My husband gave me my trench coat for Christmas after I'd lived in Manhattan for twenty-three years and been married to him for fifteen years. I wore it with everything: jeans and white shirt; a dress and high heels. And then I reached into a closet—at a friend's house or at bridge club or at Elizabeth Arden's Red Door Salon—and put on another woman's coat and walked straight out the door.

No, I didn't notice right away. I noticed within the week. It didn't smell like me (Chanel's Sycamore, peppermints, and a faint whiff of cats). It was shorter, I'm sure of it. It was snug in the bust. And then there was the issue of the buckle, which I tried to convince myself that I was remembering wrong. My diagnosis: menopause was upon me like a panther in the night. Hot flash: in less than a week, I'd gained weight and lost my mind.

But I did my due diligence. I emailed my friend Carolyn, who'd hosted a dinner party.

April 2, 2017

Subject: Weird question

Me: By any chance did I take your Burberry overcoat out of your closet instead of mine?

Carolyn: Nope, I still have mine.

Me: I think I must be going crazy. I've been walking around thinking I'm in someone else's coat. Hmmm.

Carolyn: Remember on your way out the door from my apt. you said you were able to tell your trench by the hair dye marks near the collar? You at least left my apt. with your trench . . .

This is true about the hair dye. I dry-clean my trench coat—not because of city streets and subway seats, but because of my ring around the collar. But, again, this is Manhattan: forty-and-older brunettes are as common as monogrammed SUVs in the South. I visited Vermont recently and was shocked by the silver heads that dotted the Mad River Valley like thistles. A friend told me Alaska is also like this: full of wild-haired women. You do not see gray hair on the Upper East Side. Salt and pepper is for the dinner table. Women like me will give up rent-controlled apartments before we go back to our roots.

I emailed my friend Terri, who'd hosted our bridge group.

April 3, 2017
Subject: Weird question

Me: By any chance did I take your Burberry overcoat out of your closet instead of mine?

Terri: No.

Terri (a day later): Did you find your coat?

Me: NO and I am positive I'm wearing someone else's.

I retraced my steps and no other woman had reported that she'd walked away with the wrong coat. So, I took the trench (that wasn't my trench) to the good dry cleaner. "The good dry cleaner" is Southern Lady Code for *the one that costs so much you rip off the receipt before you open the plastic bag, then crumple that receipt like a dirty Polaroid and cover it with cat litter in the garbage can because you are so ashamed of how much you spent*. The good dry cleaner made the trench look brand new. I wore it until it started to smell like me, but it still felt wrong. Every time I put it on, it felt like a lie. I felt like a thief. I was in someone else's skin. Or I was the tiniest bit of a lunatic. The coat did not spark joy.

My husband asked, "Do you want to give it to Goodwill and buy another one?"

"No," I said. Believing I was wearing another woman's trench coat was one thing, but giving it away and buying a new one would *really* be crazy. The Case of the Mistaken Trench Coat is not a mystery that should be solved.

This is the way I handle a lot of problems that are not real problems. Aka: Rich people problems. I'm lucky to have the life that I have, so my motto is: Oh, it's fine.

I don't send food back in a restaurant unless there's a finger in it. There's never a finger in it, so I don't send food back. Oh, it's fine. If the chicken breast is as pink as a prom corsage, I just don't eat it. I pay for it, unless the waiter offers to take it off the bill.

When I sold my short story collection, I took a chunk of the advance to redo our bathroom. This included wallpaper, tiles, fixtures, and plumbing. We kept the floor (original), tub (huge), and toilet (tank-free with a flush as strong as a riptide). But the tile went up wrong. The contractor picked a harsh grout, so it scratched all the tiles. The tile was redone, and I was pleased until my husband shut the door to christen the bathroom and I heard him say what you never want to hear your husband say behind a closed bathroom door: "Uh-oh."

The second round of tile had been put up without shaving back the walls, so the walls stuck out so far that the toilet lid hit the wall and wouldn't stay up on its own. To boot: the plumber installed the shower knobs backward.

I said, "Oh, it's fine," which in this instance was Southern Lady Code for *I'm not going to have them redo this a third time, the room* looks *gorgeous (who cares if it's not 100 percent functional?), let's just get on with our lives.*

My husband and I live with such problems (undercooked chicken and a toilet lid that he holds up with one knee) because these are the kinds of problems that we want to have. We've faced real problems. My husband watched his parents die. The two of us watched his brother and grandmother die. I was raped. So what if I'm wearing another woman's Burberry trench coat? I mean, really? It really is fine.

But I did worry that I might be wrong about the coat being the wrong coat. Going crazy would be a real problem.

For my forty-seventh birthday, my husband walked me to the Burberry store on East 57th Street. A saleswoman escorted us to the second floor and the first thing I noticed about the wall of trench coats was that none of them have metal buckles. They all had plastic or leather buckles (I still can't figure out the material).

I said, "It's official: I've lost my mind."

My husband said, "No, you were right about the buckle. I didn't know it at the time, but I bought you a coat from their cheaper line. The bright side is that it seems you traded up and someone else got the cheap coat."

I looked at myself in the mirror, wrapped in the other woman's Burberry coat. Identical coats hung on display. I said, "I can't trade this coat for the same coat."

"But you hate wearing it," my husband said. "Just try some on."

The saleswoman, who'd been listening to our conversation as if she heard The Case of the Mistaken Trench

Coat every day, sprang into action. She brought me three cuts of tan trench coats. I tried them on but felt like a fool.

My husband said, "Maybe try a different color."

The saleswoman showed me the trenches in black.

My husband said, "Any other color?"

The saleswoman excused herself to the storeroom. She came back with a trench coat in a color that would never sell in Manhattan, so they didn't keep it on the sales floor. On the Upper East Side, women wear black and tan. Except they call tan *camel*. And camel-colored anything is synonymous with chic. I'd wanted to be chic. I'd wanted to own a timeless fashion staple. The coat in the saleswoman's hands was a bright paperclip.

The trench was royal blue. It's a color Mama wore when she went to law school at forty. It is very Delta Burke, circa *Designing Women*. I slipped it on and the royal blue turned my pale skin to porcelain. I blinked and my eyes were sapphires. I was in love, but I wouldn't blend in.

We bought it anyway. It cost $1,895.

My husband said, "It's an investment piece."

After seventeen years of marriage, my husband is fluent in Southern Lady Code. An "investment piece" is Southern Lady Code for *costs more than a bedroom set, but you'll wear it for decades*. For me, it's an insurance policy. I'll never again take another woman's coat by mistake.

PEGGY SUE GOT

MARIJUANA

The first time I saw marijuana was in the movie *9 to 5*. I was ten years old, and Dolly Parton, Lily Tomlin, and Jane Fonda had been done wrong by the boss and were commiserating with an old-fashioned ladies' pot party. They shared a joint, savored leftovers, and hallucinated feminism. This looked—and still looks—like great fun to me. Would I like to lasso, hogtie, and roast *a sexist, egotistical, lying, hypocritical bigot* over a spit? All while wearing cowboy boots and fringed suede? Why, yes. Yes, I would.

But I am not a lady who knows how to get pot. And I am not the kind of lady to whom pot is offered. I don't look like a pothead. What does a pothead look like? Somewhere between a Jamaican glass-bottom boat driver and Susan Sarandon.

I've been to Jamaica, I went to college in Boulder, Colorado, and I moved to New York City at twenty-two but was never offered pot because I looked so preppy you'd guess my tramp stamp was a monogram.

In the early nineties, I worked at Talbots on the Upper East Side and had access to a bottomless pit of hair bow clips. A hair bow clip is a Southern lady's tiara. It's made of stiff ribbon, brightly colored, and is as fat as a titmouse. Back then the whole country was wearing them, and there was a theory that you could judge a woman's IQ by where she fastened her hair bow clip: the higher the hair bow clip, the lower the IQ. I wore my hair bow clip at the nape of my neck. Still, if you saw me from behind, you'd think I'd been tagged with a tracking device.

One night after work, my friend Patti and I raced home to watch TV. We ran out of the subway and barreled down the streets toward our apartment on East Twenty-Sixth. When we broke through a clump of Rastafarians, one called after me, "Watch it, Peggy Sue!"

See, nobody offers pot to Peggy Sue.

My friend Patti also looks like Peggy Sue. Peggy Sues used to wear poodle skirts and cardigans, and then we wore hair bow clips and cardigans, and now we wear Alex and Ani charm bangle bracelets and peasant blouses. Or cardigans. We travel in pairs or in packs and, no matter our age, look like we're straight outta composition class. We're gigglers. We look like good girls. And nobody thinks we want to get high.

But we do. We just don't know how.

I'm not a smoker. I've never been able to whistle and I've never been able to inhale. When I whistle, my breath is as quiet as a bunny poot; and when I suck a cigarette, I hack like a cat coughing up a hairball. And then coughing up another one. I don't know what I'm doing wrong, all I know is I'm not doing it right.

And once you've had trouble doing something you thought you wanted to do, you quit wanting to do it. I'd like to be a lady who cliff dives and *wanders lonely as a cloud that floats on high o'er vales and hills,* but I ass-flopped from Rick's Café in Negril and crash-landed in a hot air balloon. So, these things are not for me. They're not in my wheelhouse. "Wheelhouse" is Southern Lady Code for *comfort zone*. A comfort zone is inside the box. And here's what no one is telling you about living inside the box: it's nice in here. There are Snuggies and Klondike bars.

I've been successfully high one time, thanks to my friend Patti, who moved from Manhattan to Denver, where pot is now legal. Patti does not do pot, but she is my best friend and an excellent hostess. So at forty-four, I went to visit her.

In broad daylight on Halloween, she drove me to a

distillery that looked like a Starbucks. Two middle-aged ladies sat in a reception area wearing skinny head-bands with alien antennas. They took our middle-aged lady drivers' licenses and buzzed us through a door, where pot was laid out in every form: houseplants, fudge globs, sticky rice, and candy. No, I don't think these are the proper terms for what I saw, but I'm Peggy Sue, not Procter & Gamble.

I bought what looked like two Jolly Ranchers for under five dollars. I had one of them while Patti's husband took their son trick-or-treating. Patti laid out a charcuterie for parents who brought their kids by her house. While she socialized, I manned the front door and gave out chocolate bars.

Here's what I remember about being high: every kid's costume was freaking fantastic and I made love to a box of super seed crackers. I was relaxed and happy and very much in the moment. It was one of the best nights of my life.

I didn't have the nerve to smuggle home the other Jolly Rancher (which as far as I know is still in Patti's panty drawer), but apparently it's pretty easy for Peggy Sues. What you do is: put the pot candy in a bag of regular look-alike candy and put that bag in your carry-on luggage. If you have a kid, slip it in *your kid's* carry-on luggage. No TSA agent will give a lady who looks like Patti or me a second look. Which makes me wonder why drug cartels don't recruit bridge players, mall walkers, and that society of women who wear red hats and purple clothes. They should troll college drop-offs for moms. Empty nesters are up for adventure. And nobody pats down Peggy Sue.

Which is why I have no fear of writing about my flirtation with pot. Nobody's going to arrest me for flirting. And that's all it was: flirting.

My friends know I'm a flirt. And God bless them, after years of giving me jam jars and forty-five-dollar candles, two of them came up with an original hostess gift. At one party, I carried my first marijuana cigarette, tied with a ribbon, around all night in my apron pocket. I flashed it at guests like a nipple pastie but never smoked it because I can't smoke. I sealed it in a sandwich bag, put it in *my* panty drawer, and tossed it a year later because, despite my best efforts, it had gone stale. I don't know how to test marijuana cigarettes for freshness, but it was as brittle as a vanilla bean and I don't think that's good. I got a second joint as a gift and tried to smoke it in front of lawyer friends who've committed a good portion of their lives to sending drug dealers to prison. They were not pleased with me, but I thought of it as if I'd put a lampshade over my head. It's all in good fun in the privacy of my own home. I'm not hurting anyone. *Look everyone, Peggy Sue's gone wild!* And by wild, I mean she's looking at you kinda funny.

This year, my husband gave me a vape pen for Valentine's Day. He ordered it through a friend like I order Girl Scout cookies. The pen came in three parts like a dollhouse pool cue. You screw them together and charge the pen in your laptop USB port. It's supposed to be easier to inhale from than a rolled cigarette. It's supposed to give you a better high because it's juice, not leaves, and whatever makes you paranoid is strained out like pulp. Again, I have no idea what I am talking about. I might as well be explaining how my hair curlers get hot.

My husband's friend told him, "It's not your college marijuana. Take one hit. Just take one hit. If you start to freak out, wait twenty minutes and you'll mellow."

My husband has no interest in pot but gets a kick out of the fact that I'm trying to introduce it into my life like vegetables and tennis. He pressed a little blue button on the vape pen until it lit up and then handed it to me. I took a drag, dove into a heart-shaped box of Russell Stover cream centers, and laughed for two minutes when he shouted an answer at *Family Feud*. No, I don't remember what one hundred married men were surveyed about, but my husband answered: "The scrotum, Steve!"

A friend, whom I'll call Pseudonym Lily, said, "You didn't do it right."

I said, "How do you know?"

She said, "Bring it to my place. I've got the apartment to myself this weekend. I'll invite Pseudonym Judy and we'll show you how."

Pseudonym Lily and Pseudonym Judy were potheads in college. Pseudonym Lily smoked every day for four years. Pseudonym Judy's boyfriend gave her a bong with a gas mask. Now they play mah-jongg and needlepoint. They look like Peggy Sues. But they are not Peggy Sues.

Pseudonym Judy said, "You're doing it wrong. You're supposed to hold the blue circle down and inhale until the blue circle goes off."

I do this and the pen crackles. The mouthpiece warms up. The smoke is hot in my mouth and my lungs burn.

"Hold it," said Pseudonym Lily.

"Hold it," said Pseudonym Judy.

"Now, blow it out slowly. It should come out in a straight line. If it comes out in a puff, you're doing it wrong."

I blew out a straight line.

"Nice!"

"Good job!"

And then I felt what it was supposed to feel like. My body melted. I felt faint, but I didn't faint. I ate cheese. I ate cheese. I ate a baby carrot. We laughed. They talked and I tried to keep up. I didn't speak. We laughed. Did I mention the cheese? It was a very *9 to 5* old-fashioned ladies' pot party. And then four hours passed and it was time to go home.

WHAT EVERY GIRL

SHOULD LEARN FROM

ABC'S *THE BACHELOR*

No fairy tale begins: "Once upon a time, he blind-folded me in the back of a car." No fantasy suite has another woman's hair clogging the drains. A suitcase full of gowns doesn't make you a princess. Be careful what you wish for, Cinderella's house was infested with mice.

If a man doesn't kiss you, he doesn't want to kiss you. If a man doesn't kiss you on the mouth, he doesn't find you attractive. A fist bump is not a kiss. An ass pat is not a kiss. Don't trust a man who keeps your kisses a secret.

When a man asks you to "Put your heart out there," he means: *take off your top and get in a Jacuzzi*.

When a man puts *his* heart out there, he leaves the bathroom door open.

Classy women wear one-pieces. Smart women think

on balconies. The clearer the ocean, the cloudier the mind. Indecision *is* a decision. Patience is a curling iron in 100 percent humidity. Throw blankets signify the good life. Ladies who seem like they never have a bad day occasionally have *a very, very bad* day. Sex is like a funny cat video: everyone thinks theirs is special, but we've all fallen off a couch.

Don't forgive a man who repeatedly hurts your feelings. Don't choose a man by how you think he'll treat your kids *once you have kids*. If a man won't tell you where you're going on a date, you're camping. If a man calls his dog's name before yours, well *dang*.

Just because a man is the first to tell you he loves you doesn't mean he loves you the most.

Sometimes your second choice is the best choice.

A good man is like a pair of bargain bin pricey panties: snatch him up first, and ignore tiny flaws later. You could do a lot worse than a poet who plays baseball and is in line to take over his dad's chiropractor business. Forget helicopters and exotic locations. It's easy to fall in love on a front porch under an American flag.

THE GHOST EXPERIENCE

I t was a Friday night in Manhattan and I was home with two friends. There was watercress dip and a bottle of wine, an LED swing lamp, and five hundred puzzle pieces of a spooky owl in midflight. My friend Megan writes bestselling mystery novels. My friend Dani reads incessantly. Both women jigsaw. And puzzling women are open to anything. For example, Dani wore yoga pants to work a jigsaw puzzle. My idea of child's pose is crouching over a box top. Megan wore a cardigan, which we Southern ladies consider active wear.

Megan asked, "Has either of you ever had a ghost experience?"

Before Dani could answer no, I answered, "Who hasn't?"

Megan said, "I was in Chicago having drinks at a hotel

bar. All of a sudden I got a chill and smelled bleach. I thought I was going to faint, and I didn't want to do it in public, so I left the bar and went to my room."

"Of course you did," said Dani, plucking out edge pieces like other women pluck red jelly beans out of a jar.

I said, "The last time I fainted I did it on a bus. I peed a little."

Dani said, "My husband passed out in a men's room last week. He gets overheated. They called an ambulance, and I walked into the emergency room shouting, 'Where's my husband? He's totally fine!'"

Megan said, "So I'm in my hotel room and I get the ice bucket. When I open the door to go get ice, there's a man in front of my door. Just standing there. Right in front of my door. He's tall and thin and old and pale and dressed like something out of the past. He's wearing a hat. And he's just standing there. Staring at me."

"Did you shut the door?" I ask.

"No, I was somehow already out in the hallway with my door closed behind me. All I could think to do was ask him where the ice machine was."

"Of course you did," said Dani. She plucked out an owl eye.

Megan said, "He pointed down the hall in this weird slow-motion way."

"And you went?" I asked.

"Of course she did," said Dani, and plucked out a beak.

"But that's a closed environment," I said. "A second location. Oprah says, Don't let them take you to a second location. Did he follow you?"

Dani finally looked up.

"No," said Megan. "When I got to the end of the hall, he was somehow at the other end. He's at one end and I'm at the other. And that's when I see that there's no vending machine room. I'm standing in front of a glass door that leads to a gym. And I'm frozen, thinking: do I go in here? And he holds up his hand and makes a gesture, again real slow, moving his hand back and forth like an Egyptian, like slide your key in. And I do it because I'm so freaked out."

"Is anyone in the gym?" I ask.

"No, it's totally empty. So I just stand in there with all the treadmills, holding my empty ice bucket until a woman walks in to work out, sees me, and screams."

"Of course she does!" screamed Dani.

"I know!" screamed Megan.

I asked, "Which one was the ghost?"

"What do you mean?" asked Dani. "The man was the ghost."

"Where I come from," I said, "three things could be ghosts: the chill and the bleach smell, the man, and the woman. Just because a woman's wearing mesh capris doesn't mean she's not a ghost. People die nowadays too, you know. All ghosts aren't going be in tuxedos and nightgowns."

———

The first ghost who visited me wore a black flared skirt, a black suit jacket, a tailored white blouse, and black one-inch heels. Mama says she remembers the shoes in particular.

Mama says, "I was looking down on you while you were sleeping, and I saw the black shoes by the foot of your crib. I looked up and there was this woman. She was just standing there. Looking down at you, too. So I ran out and hollered, 'There's a woman in Helen Michelle's room!' Your father—never one to ask questions in a crisis—flew up the steps and found no one in the nursery. He checked the whole house and found no one."

In all the times I've heard this story, not once has the experience been attributed to postpartum depression, one too many whiskey sours, or sleep deprivation. Mama was not hallucinating. There was a ghost in my room.

At first, Mama wished it was her mother, who'd died a few months earlier. Later, she admitted the ghost's face was unrecognizable and that in all honesty she couldn't imagine her mother wearing something so drab, so it could have been someone who died on the property.

Then, for a while, she thought it was a nun. Mama's side of the family is Catholic and has been in the South since 1738. Like some families have politicians, we've got nuns.

We also have ghosts. There's the story about Great-aunt Belle, whose perfume drifted through the house at her funeral reception. Our great-great-grandmother's dog dug a grave the night her husband died at sea. Mama's parents loved ghosts so much, on Halloween they'd throw on bedsheets and sit in the shrubbery to horrify trick-or-treaters.

Mama laughs. "Oh, Helen Michelle, there was a lot of pee-pee on our porch!"

Papa's side of the family does not have ghosts. Or, as he's said, "They aren't something we spoke about."

Like other families don't admit to Darwin's theory of evolution or diabetes.

But Papa has never contradicted Mama. On any parenting choice. He supported her decision to raise my sister and me as tomboy artistic feminist hoots. And he let us be raised to believe in ghosts.

Elizabeth and I grew up in a haunted house. In an otherwise happy home—where Alabama football was on the TV in the den and Little Debbie snack cakes were overstocked in the kitchen cupboards—there were two rooms that frightened us.

Elizabeth says, "The living room was pure evil."

I say, "I still get the creeps when I see eighties pastels."

The living room was to the right of the front door. It had the good couch. It had my father's four-piece stereo set. It's where the Christmas tree went. It was the one room in the house that the neighbors could see free and clear from the street. And my parents were proud of it. So every morning, they opened the four sets of shutters. And every night, it was my sister's or my job to shut them on the way up the stairs to our bedrooms.

But by then it was dark. And the living room was even darker. And on the other side of the windows were things waiting to get in. Some people have outside cats, we had outside ghosts.

Both my sister and I—for our entire adolescence and without discussing it with each other—shut the shutters with our eyes shut. Five steps in, knees on the couch, hands on the shutters. *Shut, shut, shut,* and *shut.* Get out. Once you see a face in a window, you don't want to see it again.

Directly above the living room was my sister's room. She had three closets, and inside one of them was a tiny door. The tiny door looked like it had been cut out of the sheetrock with a chainsaw. Instead of a knob, it had a turn latch hammered in with a nail. The tiny door led to an attic. And something existed inside of that attic. When we heard it go bump in broad daylight, not once did we ever think possum or squirrel.

On my sister's twelfth birthday, it came out of the closet.

She was having a sleepover and telling ghost stories. Her friends were on her bed, and Elizabeth was across the room in a rocking chair next to the closet with the tiny door. I don't remember the ghost story, but the refrain is: *Oh Mama, oh Mama, don't care for me. Chop my head off, chop my head off!* And as soon as Elizabeth said those words, she was whacked in the neck.

No, nobody saw what hit her, but there are six living witnesses who saw my sister flinch, clutch her throat, and scream. And then everyone saw that the closet door and the tiny door were open. They had opened all by themselves.

The girls ran down the stairs to our parents, hollering, "There's a ghost in Elizabeth's room!" Papa—once again, never one to ask questions—flew up the steps and found no one in my sister's room. He checked the attic and found no one. He let the slumber party sleep in the den.

My parents never followed up with a trip to a child psychologist or antianxiety medication. Elizabeth was not crying out for help or having some sort of episode. There was a ghost in her room.

And she, like me as a baby, had to live with it.

My family's attitude toward ghosts is the same that we have toward hornets' nests and noisy hotel neighbors: don't bother them and they won't bother you in a worse way than they are already bothering you. Ghosts are real. It's the South. Our homes are built on battlegrounds and centuries-old horrors. Everybody's house has some dead relative knocking around or rearranging the furniture. Got a ghost stomping across the hardwood floors and waking you up every night? Install wall-to-wall carpeting. You don't move, you make do.

———

Megan, Dani, and I were two hours into our spooky owl puzzle and working on forest leaves. Half the puzzle was forest leaves—all orange or burnt orange—so we were laying out pieces according to shape. One knob and three holes, two knobs and two holes, four holes—you get the idea: this was the hard part. But puzzling women are patient. We'll take the time to make sense out of something that's broken.

Megan said, "So, if you saw a ghost in this apartment, you'd ignore it?"

I stared over Megan's shoulder and whispered, "I'm ignoring one right now."

Dani looked up.

"Just kidding!" I said. "But seriously, there are a lot of ghosts in the building. It's a hundred years old. People die. There've been four suicides I know about: gunshot, bathtub, and two jumped out the windows. All the doormen have seen ghosts. And there's a haunted baby carriage in the basement."

"Of course there is," said Dani.

I said, "It's straight out of *Rosemary's Baby*. It moves between storage bins when nobody's watching. One day it's by the laundry machines, the next day it's by the boiler. The super doesn't know who it belongs to, but refuses to throw it out. My husband says there was a ghost right here where we puzzle."

"What do you mean *right here where we puzzle*?" asked Dani.

"I mean, like, right here. There's always been a dining table in this spot, and before my husband was born, his brother Kip saw a woman in a ball gown standing next to it. She was blond and wore her hair up. She wore jewelry and opera gloves. Kip called her the Moon Lady."

"Did your husband ever see her?" asked Megan.

"No."

"But he believes she was here?"

"Of course he does," said Dani.

I hated to admit it: "No, he doesn't."

———

My sister went so far as to make her California husband swear to believe in ghosts in their wedding vows: *Stefan, do you promise to love Elizabeth for who she is now and who she will become, to encourage her Southernness and to hold her hand, especially when things are scary? Do you promise to live in a big old house with cats and dogs and kids and secret passageways and to have a wraparound porch where you can sit and watch the thunderstorms? Do you promise to say "okay" and move out without question if she tells you the house is haunted?*

He did.

When their daughter, Katy Belle (who was named after Great-aunt Belle), spoke to the People in the Fireplace at four years old, and then at six woke to see a man drink a grape soda in her bedroom, and then at seven asked my sister if ghosts are real and Elizabeth said, "Oh, yes, we are a family that *likes* ghosts!" Stefan didn't contradict her. He is helping to raise a funny intelligent feminist glamazon.

What I didn't tell Megan and Dani is: I *have* seen a ghost in our apartment.

The last ghost I saw was my husband's brother, Kip.

Kip died of a brain aneurism at twenty-nine. More than twenty years ago, I woke to find him sitting between us in bed. Kip was in Converse sneakers, 501 jeans, and a T-shirt. He was just sitting there. Looking straight ahead, with a hand on my husband and me.

When I eventually told my husband that I had seen his brother, he didn't ask questions. We haven't moved. And he's never asked if I've seen Kip again. He accepts my story. I think he likes that I believe. Like he likes that I do puzzles. While my husband doesn't want to do either—see ghosts or work a jigsaw—he appreciates that I include him in both odd parts of my life.

But for now, my ghosts are gone.

And my one rule of puzzle night is: after my friends and I put together five hundred to one thousand parts of a picture, my husband gets to put in the last piece. My friends don't object. Puzzling women are generous. We want everyone to share in our experiences.

PARTY FOUL

I n 1983, my parents threw a Halloween birthday party for me and thirty other eighth graders in a one-room round house in the middle of a park. The house was one story, one room, walled off, with no windows. It had a glass-door entrance and—as well as I or anyone else can remember—no back exit. Was it a safety hazard? Well, of course it was, but that was part of the fun. If a candle fell off my cake, we would go up like a trash can fire. It was dark outside, everyone's parents had dropped them off, and the nearest civilization was a Taco Casa drive-thru miles and miles away.

For costumes my friend Vicki and I dressed up as punk rockers, which to us meant side ponies and T-shirts with safety pins in the necks. My friend Liz came as the Grim Reaper in a black hooded robe with a four-foot-long sickle she'd crafted from Reynolds Wrap. My friend Ellen greased her short black hair and came as Ralph "Let's do it for Johnny!" Macchio from *The Outsiders*. My friend Laura came as Trixie, a "lady of the night," which meant she wore a feather boa. But none of the boys paid us any attention because of what the one early-developed girl wore.

"Early-developed" is Southern Lady Code for *brace face and B cups*. This girl wore a flesh-colored leotard and wrapped a nine-foot-long stuffed carnival snake around her body like a roller-coaster tattoo.

"Her mother escorted her in, carrying the tail," Mama remembers. "And what could we say? We were in the Bible Belt after all, why wouldn't she come as Eve?"

My parents had threatened to dress up as Tweedledee and Tweedledum, topped off with propeller beanies. They'd thought this would be hilarious. I'd thought it would be mortifying. So they wore jeans, as did a twenty-three-year-old female classmate of Mama's. Mama was in her forties but had just entered law school. Nothing embarrassed her.

One of Mama's parenting mantras was: "Oh, Helen Michelle, I have *yet to begin* to embarrass you."

I have no memory of what we did for the first half of my birthday party. I remember eating pizza at cafeteria-style tables with the stools attached when Papa turned off the lights.

He rolled out a cart with a TV the size of a convection oven. The electrical cord dangled off the back, the prongs barely scraping the floor. So, the TV went where the wall outlet was. One group of kids collectively stood and scooted their table closer for a better view.

Papa slipped a tape into the VCR and announced that we'd be watching a scary movie. "*Cat People* starring Nastassja Kinksi," he said as if the Tuscaloosa Blockbuster rivaled Cannes in the South of France.

I have no memory of how far we made it into that movie. I couldn't tell you who else was in it or if any of them actually turned into cats. All I remember is that the movie was black and white, and at some point my friend Laurie, dressed like Coco from *Fame* in legwarmers and a ballet skirt, reached over to the TV knob and switched it off.

Something was happening to our left, just inside the round house by the glass door.

A man was yelling at Mama's classmate. He was a stranger. He was bearded. He held a wallet. It was not his wallet. It was another man's wallet. He shouted that he'd found the wallet, *another man's* wallet, under their bed. So, this man was married to Mama's friend and she had cheated on him.

And he was furious.

How furious?

He shouted, "If I can't have you, nobody can!"

And then he pulled out a gun.

It was a handgun, which he didn't hold over his head like a warning. He pointed that gun straight at his wife, who backed toward Mama.

She said, "No, no. Please. No, please, no no no, don't do it."

Mama, I will never forget, looked the gunman straight in the face, put her hands on her hips, and said, "You are *ruining* my daughter's party!"

Talk about rude. Threatening to murder your wife in public was a far worse social offense than dropping an unwrapped Baby Ruth bar into a punch bowl.

"I'm gonna kill you!" the man roared at his wife. "I'm gonna kill you!"

But none of us Alabama eighth graders ran.

We melted off our stools and slid under the tables. A few years later in high school a kid would pull a gun at lunch and we would again melt under the same kind of tables in exactly the same way.

Laurie remembers being the last one standing at my party. She emailed me recently, "I was staring at the dude with the gun and watching the whole thing, wondering what happened to him that he got to this point? Like from a thirteen-year-old's perspective, so basically: WHY ARE YOU SO MESSED UP? And then I also remember someone tugging on me to get DOWN. Was it you, Helen?"

It was me. Because cower is what you did when you saw a man with a weapon.

Every man we knew carried a weapon.

Our principals patrolled the halls with wooden paddles. Some drilled holes in the inch-thick wood in shop class so the paddles whistled when they swung. One vice principal never sat because he kept a yardstick down the inside back leg of his pants. We'd all been threatened or spanked at school or hit at home with a switch or a belt.

And everyone's parents had guns.

To this day, there's a semiautomatic, double-stack 9mm Beretta in Papa's nightstand and .380 Sig Sauer in his car. Not to mention the revolvers and pistols he purchased or inherited from his father that he will pass on to my sister and me. What I will do with them when I get them I do not know. "It's an heirloom" is Southern Lady Code for *cold steel and ammunition*.

Papa raised us with the knowledge: "If you find a gun, it's loaded."

Guns are not toys. You don't play with guns. If you point a gun at someone, you've already fired it. If someone pulls a gun on you, you don't turn your back and run and make yourself a target.

Kids were crying under the tables.

Laurie says, "I remember somebody *really* crying. Like hard, hard, hard."

Me, I remember doing the math: A gun has six bullets, there are thirty-three of us. I remember my judgment: if Mama's friend wasn't such a slut, this wouldn't be happening. And I remember looking to Papa: *How are you going to save us?*

Laura remembers, "The guy pointed the gun at your dad."

And Papa said, "Let's take it outside."

He opened the glass door and the man followed him out.

Only Mama and the young woman were at a vantage point to see through the glass door. The rest of us crouched in darkness.

And then there was quiet.

And then there were gunshots.

And then Mama screamed. She pointed at what she saw through the glass door and screamed so loud and so long that I swear, decades later, my ears are still ringing.

And I thought: *My father is dead.*

And then, there he was: Papa bounding into the round house with the gunman. The gunman was smiling. His wife and my parents were smiling. Papa said, "Okay, listen up, kids! We're gonna break you into teams of five and see who can remember the most about what just happened!"

Mama passed out legal pads and pens.

It had all been a joke. Papa had hired two actors from

the University of Alabama for twenty-five dollars apiece and staged the whole thing.

And now we kids were crawling out from under the tables, wiping our faces, and scribbling furiously.

Laura remembers, "It was a game to test our observation skills. We were supposed to see how good we would be as a 'witness' if it had been an actual crime. One boy on my team acted like he knew it was a game all along, he said the guy had once come to one of our acting classes, so he knew it was fake. But I didn't remember the guy or think it was a game."

Me, I don't remember who was on my team or what first place was. I don't remember prize-winning details like the gunman's eye color or whether his wife's jeans were Jordache or Gloria Vanderbilt.

But I do remember Liz, aka the Grim Reaper, said, "Mr. Ellis, you're going to pay for my therapy."

But her parents never made an appointment for her with a shrink.

And nobody's parents sued us, the cops weren't called, and the gun was real.

Papa remembers, "The gun was one of mine. It was loaded with blank cartridges. In other words, it could only make a loud noise and not hurt someone even if pointed right at them. Real bullets would have been too dangerous."

Hey, some fathers take their girls to daddy-daughter

dances or buy them puppies; my father faked his own death for my birthday.

For my sixteenth birthday, Papa convinced me I was seventeen. He said, "Helen Michelle, have you ever *seen* your birth certificate?"

For my seventeenth birthday, he rented a white Econoline van, the trademark of a serial killer. I don't remember which serial killer, but I remember that if you saw a white van idling at your curb like an ice cream truck, you were supposed to run away like it was doling out double scoops of Mint Chocolate Razor Blades. Anyhoo, my parents drove that white van and "kidnapped" my friends to come celebrate with me.

Mama says, "Oh, Helen Michelle, there was a lot of kicking and screaming going on in some driveways!"

Mama finally quit finding Papa's practical jokes funny when he called her from an airport pay phone to say that my little sister was missing. He said, "Don't panic. But I've lost her."

And then he had my sister call from a pay phone right beside him and cry, "Mama, heeeelp!"

On the drive home from my thirteenth birthday party, I was mortified, but Papa laughed off my teenage despair as if the prank he'd pulled was no more embarrassing than a whoopee cushion or dribble glass. He thought I should be thanking him. He had my best interest at heart.

He said, "Next year, when you start high school, everyone's going to know who you are."

And they did.

"And they're all gonna want to hear about that party."

And they did.

Folks still do.

Laura, aka Trixie, says, "It's been one of the stories I tell people now, and they can't believe it happened. If it were 2019 instead of 1983, it would've gone viral, made national news, and had a lawsuit or two sprinkled in."

Ellen, aka Ralph "Stay Gold" Macchio says, "I wasn't a fan of Halloween then and I'm *really* not now. And I thought I came as Pony Boy. *Outsiders* rule!"

Me, I'm still friends with all of these women, who despite Papa's practical jokes, turned out okay. All of us are married. Three of us have kids and three of us chose not to. But we all stay home on Halloween night. We hold the candy bowls. We look through our peepholes. Because sometimes, under exactly the right circumstances, we like to be scared.

TODAY WAS A GOOD DAY!

There wasn't a clown in my closet. A doll did not turn its head to look at me. A music box did not start playing on its own. A pair of shoes wasn't sticking out from beneath my drapes. A man in a hazmat suit didn't knock on my door. A snake didn't jack-in-the-box out of my toilet. A hair on my face was not growing out of my face.

No one said: "Keep still, this'll be over before you know it."

No one asked, "You're not from around these parts, are you?"

No one said, "Bless you!" when I sneezed alone in my home.

No one slapped me across the face and told me to relax.

I didn't yank oxygen tubes out of my nose. I didn't back out of a room slowly. I didn't crawl through an air duct. I didn't chop off and bleach my hair in a gas station restroom. I didn't carve a pistol out of soap. I didn't burn off my own fingerprints. I didn't make a rope out of bedsheets. I didn't sit on a suitcase on the shoulder of a highway. I wasn't abducted by a "weather balloon."

I didn't fall to my knees and scream, "Noooooo!"

I didn't raise my hands toward the heavens and scream, "Whyyyyyy?"

I didn't ask, "Was none of it true?"

I didn't answer, "What in the world were you thinking?"

I didn't dump my purse over the head of someone texting in a movie theater. I didn't dump my purse over the head of someone texting in a movie theater *again*. I didn't windmill my arms into a fistfight. I didn't act as my own attorney. I didn't draw straws in prison. I didn't pick the lesser of two evil tattoos. I didn't cut out newspaper articles, tape them to a wall, and connect them with red string. I didn't reenter society.

I didn't say, "You don't know me!"

I didn't say, "There's someone in here!"

I didn't say, "There is too a ghost!"

I didn't say, "What's the worst that could happen?"

I didn't choke on a cupcake for breakfast. I didn't bleed out from a Cling Wrap serrated edge. I didn't reach into a bag of chips and get bit. I didn't make a deal with the Dirt Devil and get my soul sucked out by a vacuum cleaner.

STRAIGHTEN UP AND

FLY RIGHT

Congratulations, you are sitting next to the most considerate person on the plane. Seat 17B, that's me. I'll fly for up to four hours in this middle seat with my arms pinched to my sides and this mass-market paperback book in my hands. Yes, the print is tiny, but that's why I wore my glasses. I've sacrificed my vanity to make you, Seat 17C, and this guy by the window in 17A more comfortable.

By the way, before you got here, 17A and I took a vote and closed the shade. The reason I have no fear of flying is that I imagine myself a parrot in a cage under a blanket. Polly wants sensory deprivation! What's there to see once we're up in the air anyway? Clouds. Crop circles. Been there, done that.

17A is already asleep. Isn't he darling? His head lolls

on his neck pillow like a ball-in-cup game. As soon as he sat down and we finished exchanging the same pleasantries that I'm exchanging with you, he drugged himself "with something expired he found in his dead father's medicine cabinet." He's not going to disturb us (or anyone else) until after we land and someone shakes him like a can of paint.

Pardon me for saying so, but you might have thought to check your carry-on bag.

Honestly, nobody wants to help you put your bag in the overhead bin. Nobody wants to watch you hoist your bag like a sack of bricks and Barbies onto your seat back, then onto your clavicle, and then into the overhead bin. No, your bag won't fit that way. It goes wheels out. Now you've got a stewardess involved. I mean flight attendant. I mean woman who wants you to—as a Delta employee once begged on my flight out of Atlanta—"Put your *tush* in the *cush* so we can *push*."

What's so bad about waiting ten minutes for your bag to come through on the carousel? I'd rather wait by the carousel than wait in a hot metal tube that smells like Chick-fil-A. What are you so afraid to lose? You can fit your tube top in your purse.

Neatly. You *roll* a tube top.

9F's handbag looks like a laundry sack. It wouldn't fit under the seat in front of her, so now a flight attendant is carrying the sack like it fainted and trolling the overhead bins for a hole. 9F is Facebook live-streaming the flight attendant, who is just doing her job. 9F is going to get herself kicked off this flight and delay our departure.

My handbag sits stiff and obedient under the seat in front of me like a magician's top hat. It has many secret compartments that hold many secret things. If this plane goes down on a deserted island, I'll be the last one to sunburn (SPF 50), get sick (Airborne), or eat the pilot (peanut M&M's). Worried about terrorism and can't get through security with 3.4 ounces of pepper spray? A knee sock and a roll of quarters goes unnoticed through an X-ray machine; swing it like a chain mace, and you've got yourself one hell of a weapon (Charles Bronson in *Death Wish*).

See, I told you I was considerate. We should form an alliance before takeoff. In case of emergency, 17A will never know what hit him and everyone else on this flight is too self-absorbed.

Hear that? 16A has called someone to tell him she's boarded the plane. If these are the last words she chooses to tell her significant other before possibly tumbling out of the sky to her fiery death, then 16A is a horrible lover. It's like going to bed with a man and talking dirty about your dust ruffle.

I kiss my husband good-bye before I go to the airport,

and then I call him when I get to my hotel. In between, I read my book. But he doesn't know that. A secret to our happy marriage is: I keep an air of mystery. Where am I now? Who am I talking to? Did I poison 17A? Just kidding! It's like I'm an international spy. Or an air marshal.

And I am.

Do you know how many times I've seen something and said something?

Three times. And it's about to be four.

They've made the announcement to turn off our phones, but 15D hasn't complied, so we're all going to die. I don't know how it's going to happen, but it's going to happen and we are all going to perish pointing and yelling at him.

But *you're* the one on the aisle, so go ahead and gesture to a flight attendant about how 15D is endangering us. Go on. You've seen something, now gesture something.

No? Okay, I'll do it.

Boy, that flight attendant is really laying into him; but 15D deserves it, and I'll admit I get off on watching him pay for his crime. For the rest of this flight, I'll revel in 15D's chastisement like other women might delight in a lap dance from Channing Tatum. Are you getting a contact high from sitting next to me, an everyday hero?

I'm a national treasure. I'm like a wheat penny. I may look small and out of circulation, but if we find ourselves iced into a mountain, altitude sick, and bartering for oxygen masks, I'll work. You can count on me.

The pilot says we're not taking off for another twenty-five minutes. This doesn't bother me, don't let it bother you. You didn't bring a book (or a fistful of pills like 17A), but today's planes are like day cares or hospitals: there are TVs eight inches from all of our throats. Look, they've got HBO. Find something to watch in which women have hair as long and as wavy as washboards and erections outnumber dragons and zombies.

Don't be embarrassed. We're all adults here.

Except for that crying baby. It's somewhere behind us, I don't know its seat. See how I'm not craning my neck to give an infant the stink eye. I told you I was considerate. It's not the baby's fault that it's crying. It's not the parent's fault either. Babies cry. Don't complain. No plane was ever delayed because a baby was crying. No plane ever *crashed* because a baby was crying. So, face forward and pump up the soft-core pornography volume.

The pilot is making another announcement. He's paused your candlelit sex scene (and everyone else's marathon of *The Real Housewives of Detroit Argue Next to Decorative Pillows*) to tell us we're grounded for another half hour. He's turned off the "Fasten Your Seat Belt" lights. If we need to use the restroom, now would be a good time to go.

You'll want to go to the restroom right after me. I was not put on this earth to straddle a commode. I wipe down a toilet seat like I'm giving it a tetanus shot.

I'm back. Why didn't you follow me? Did you peek out the window? Did you finger my book? Just kidding! See? I'm hilarious. My sense of humor will be a ray of sunshine if our plane death-spirals into the frozen tundra.

You know what else will be a comfort? My lips against yours. My husband has given me permission to kiss whomever I want if my plane goes down. I am the kind of woman who always imagines kissing my seatmate, be he man, woman, or child of eighteen. Let's be serious. If I'm going to be identified by my dental records or a Q-tip swab of DNA, I'll kiss a sixteen-year-old. And that sixteen-year-old will die happy and thanking me for showing him the ways of womanhood. "The ways of womanhood" is Southern Lady Code for *tongue*. So, brace yourself! Once this plane is at a ninety-degree angle, I'm going to ride you like Slim Pickens rode the bomb in *Dr. Strangelove*. Yeehaw!

I told you I'm the most considerate person to sit beside. I told 17A the same thing. If he were awake, he would confirm this.

HALLOWEEN PEOPLE

I RSVP'd yes to a Studio 54 party because I'd been to one of the host's parties before and it was my idea of a good time: me and my husband surrounded by fifty to sixty fabulous forty- to sixty-year-old gay men.

I told my husband, "I'll buy a wrap dress and do my hair like Jaclyn Smith."

My husband liked this idea.

He asked, "But what will I wear? I gave away my Mr. Kotter wig when you Marie Kondo'd the apartment."

I said, "A fat tie or baseball shirt with an iron-on? Don't worry, we'll think of something."

But we did not go to this party because I chickened out.

No matter how much I want to be, I am not a dresser-upper. Don't misunderstand. I'm put together. "Put together" is Southern Lady Code for *you can take me to church or Red Lobster and I'll fit in fine.* My closet has dresses, skirts, slacks, shirts, and blouses. I'm put together enough to know the difference between shirts and blouses. A shirt is stiff. A blouse billows. See, I'm educated, but there is a level of dress-up that reminds me of Halloween. And I don't do Halloween. I do Christmas.

In this world, there are Halloween people and Christmas people. Halloween people trick-or-treat, enter costume contests, and march in parades. Halloween people like to be seen, but Christmas people like for you to come over and see what they've done to their place. We decorate our houses. We dress up trees. I am the kind of woman who has more tree skirts than skirts. My sister makes me a new one every year to match my tree theme. See, I have tree themes. I am a Christmas person.

I want to be a Halloween person, but I don't like costumes. And, to me, a costume is anything I have to buy to attend an event: a wrap dress (Studio 54 party), a hat (Kentucky Derby party), or something that bares my upper arms (ball, benefit, or banquet). I don't want to shop for anything with a *"th"* sound on the invite either. You know, the sound Daffy Duck makes when he lisps, Youuu're dethpicable!

After the Studio 54 party, we got an invite to our friend Nicho's *fiftieth.*

I almost RSVP'd no right away because it was black tie.

Black tie is the dressiest of dressing up.

The last time I wore black tie was for Nicho's fortieth birthday party, which was black tie, but also a masked ball, which is dress-up on top of dress-up. For that, I bought a $300 red satin cocktail dress from a SoHo boutique. For my mask, I bought a pair of two-dollar black glittered sunglasses from Ricky's (a Halloween store). Party guests who'd special-ordered Mardi Gras masks from New Orleans or outbid strangers on eBay for masks from the orgy scene in *Eyes Wide Shut* said my sunglasses were cheating. They let me slide because of my red cocktail number, but I didn't ace the dress-up test. Now it's been a decade since I dressed up and I worry that if don't pick the right outfit I'll be turned away at the door.

It's happened before. At twenty-five, my husband and I were turned away at Lexington Bar & Books, which has a jacket-required dress code. I was cold and he'd wrapped his suit jacket around my shoulders. To be allowed in, they offered him one of theirs. I'm sure it was navy and nondescript, but I remember it as clownishly shameful: neon plaid and twelve sizes too large. We left.

My husband urged me to RSVP yes to Nicho's black tie party. He said, "We're not going to a restaurant; it's our friend's birthday. Nobody's going to turn us away. Come on, we can't *not* go because we don't have anything to wear."

By *we,* he meant me.

My husband owns a tuxedo. To prepare for Nicho's party, all he had to do was let out the waist an inch. Me, I had to commit to go and gamble that I could find something appropriate to wear. I'd given away my red dress because I'd honestly thought I'd never go to a formal event ever again.

My friend Karen said, "It's okay, it's not your lifestyle."

It's true. My lifestyle is writing, poker, puzzling, movies, dinner with friends, housework, and naps. If these were clues on *The $100,000 Pyramid* the answer would be "Things You Do in a Retirement Home!"

But dressing up is Karen's lifestyle. She was born and raised in New York City and tells me her grandmother used to wear cardigan sets and Ferragamos to sit in her own living room. Karen inherited clutch purses, jewelry, and furs from her grandmother. Like ghost sightings in mine, good taste runs in her family.

Having good taste is different from being put together. You can be put together, but not have good taste. But you can't have good taste and not be put together.

Women with good taste wear skinny headbands with a pair of animal ears for Halloween. This year, from the bangs up, Karen was a leopard. But that doesn't mean she's a Halloween person. Karen's apartment is decorated like Jonathan Adler's take on Versailles, so she is a Christmas person. When she offered to take me shopping, I jumped at the chance.

Karen said, "I'm a good friend, so I'll tell you what doesn't look good on you."

I reconsidered my decision.

She asked me for a budget.

I bid high: five hundred to a thousand dollars.

She said, "I'm a good sale shopper."

Karen led me into a cornstalk maze of markdown racks at Saks, and I wanted to flee. But shopping is fun for Karen. It's a special skill like cup stacking or texting two hundred characters a minute. She strolled right over and plucked a Stella McCartney burgundy velvet tuxedo jacket out of a haystack.

She said, "If we can find pants to match, what would you think about wearing this instead of a dress?"

I was instantly relieved. I'd thought black tie meant an empire-waisted Kate Winslet from *Titanic*. Something with gloves up to my armpits. Or something with feathers. If a tuxedo was okay for my husband, it should be okay for me. But the option had never crossed my mind. When did I lose my fashion sense?

I had it in 1975 on my first day of school. As proof, I keep framed photographic evidence on top of my chest of drawers. In the picture, I'm four years old and wearing a lime-green gingham jumpsuit with a ruffled collar. I have a bowl haircut and a lick-the-bowl smile. My Mary Janes are planted on shag carpeting, and I am staring straight into the camera. I have the look of Scout Finch with the confidence of a drag queen. Maybe Mama dressed me, but I am ready to walk into kindergarten like it's the House of LaBeija.

As a teenager in Alabama, the eighties were easy. You matched. You matched everything. You matched your shoe color to your clothes color. You matched your eye shadow to your top. Clinique's Black Honey lipstick went with everything, so to further accessorize you dipped your arms into wooden bangles or elastic bracelets with plastic gems. Maybe you wore a headband—not a skinny one, but one as puffy as a Shrinky Dink. The headband was fabric and matched your purse, which came with reversible slip-on covers so they could match more. It was easy. Turquoise went with turquoise. Blush went with bashful. There was a book that told you if you were a Winter, Spring, Summer, or Fall. You looked forward to dressing up for homecoming and prom.

But at some point after high school graduation, I lost my coordination.

Mama blames Boulder, Colorado.

I came home from college in a prairie skirt and Reeboks. I was a waifish, yet sporty Laura Ingalls Wilder. Mama pulled over the car on the way home from the airport to give me a talking-to. She said, "Helen Michelle, this is the South. We roll our hair and we wear lipstick."

Me, I blame the nineties. It's hard to bounce back from grunge. The grunge theory was: swimming in clothes makes you look skinny. Or: inner beauty is badass. I honestly can't remember. All I know is that after Doc Martens and flannel shirts, it's hard to wear stilettos and Spanx.

My parents are guilty of aiding and abetting my fashion crimes because they stopped dressing up when they retired. Papa, who wore three-piece suits to work, takes pride in the fact he hasn't worn a tie since. When my niece was born, Mama, who'd stopped practicing law—and with it the art of modeling Claire Huxtable–worthy ensembles—wore a cream-and-brown Christopher Walken T-shirt to the maternity ward that read MORE COWBELL!

So, is losing the will to dress up an age thing?

At casinos, I see senior citizens grazing on slot machines clad in a trend that I call *toddling*. Toddling is dressing like a toddler: clamdiggers and a cotton top, no belt, mall-walking sneakers. It's a look that says, *I give up.* Or, *I don't give a damn what anybody thinks of me anymore.* I'm not sure which. And I'm not sure whether I'm ready to grow gracefully into either.

I said to Karen, "I would *love* to wear a velvet tuxedo."

She flipped the price tag. At 40 percent off (with no

matching pants) the jacket was $921. She frowned. We checked the size. For once, I was happy that something so perfect for me was two sizes too small.

We moved on. Rack by rack, floor by floor. I tried on whatever Karen pulled for me. Nothing worked, but she was kind. A zipper didn't zip, and she said, "You have an hourglass body, not a little-boy body."

And then we found a St. John's jumpsuit. It was velvet! It was form-fitting! It was on sale for $595! I opened the dressing-room door and Karen said, "You look like Jaclyn Smith in Charlie's Angels!"

I thought we had a winner, but I wanted to make sure.

Karen took a photo and we texted it to my husband.

No answer.

So, we texted it to others. We group-sourced. Gay men liked it. Women liked it. But still no word from my husband. We put the jumpsuit on hold.

When I got home, I asked him why he didn't text back.

My husband said, "It was hard to tell how you looked from the picture."

Married to a Southern lady, my husband knows better than to say anything to me that can't be taken as a compliment. He'd never say he didn't like the way I looked. So, with the jumpsuit, it was the camera's fault. It was the overhead lighting's fault. The black velvet didn't photograph well. But I knew he didn't find it attractive.

He said, "You should wear something that shows your legs. You have a black dress, wear that."

Karen was disappointed that her pick didn't make the cut but agreed a black dress could be suitable for the party. With metallic high heels, a fun evening bag, and jewelry, I could dress it up.

I thought, *Like a Christmas tree.*

But the black dress wasn't going to be as easy as it sounded. It was long-sleeved and crew-necked. It hugged my body and was as warm as a weighted thunder blanket that soothes a nervous dog. It required my one pair of Spanx, which were parked in the back of my lingerie drawer like a chastity belt. And it was a *standing* dress, not a *sitting* dress. Nicho's party was a sit-down supper. But I resolved to wear it, because I didn't want to shop anymore.

And then, like true love in a rom-com, when I quit looking, a dress found me.

I saw it in a window. The Zara dress was black with a neon-blue shimmer. It had a plunge neck, a ruched waist, below-the-elbow sleeves, and a slit up the leg. It covered what I want covered and flattered my butt. It was from their Disco collection. If I had found it earlier, I could've worn it to the Studio 54 party. It was seventy dollars. I bought it without asking anyone's approval.

The night of Nicho's party, my husband and I strutted into a Gramercy Park private club like we owned the place. We checked our coats and climbed a winding staircase to find the guest of honor, but he was nowhere to be found because we'd walked into the wrong club. So, down the steps we went, picked up our coats, and on the way to the right club next door, I was able to laugh because I wasn't wearing shapewear.

"Do-over!" I shouted.

And as we walked into the right place, I felt like my four-year-old self.

TONIGHT WE'RE

GONNA PARTY

LIKE IT'S 1979

E very year, more than a hundred people crowd
into our two-bedroom Manhattan apartment for
a holiday party because I serve what my Alabama
grandmother served in the 1970s. Forget sushi platters.
The gluten-free can gnaw on mistletoe. I am a Southern
lady who's lived among the Upper East Side elite for my
entire middle-aged life, and here's what I've learned: If
you can't join 'em, beat 'em into submission with good
old-fashioned gooey goodness. The secret ingredient is
never love, it's mayonnaise. My days of cooking fancy to
fit in are over.

Oh, I tried in the beginning. For our first parties, I
stuffed mushrooms, blanched asparagus spears, filled
puffed pastries, and threaded marinated olives onto
toothpicks. I ran my oven at 450 degrees Fahrenheit,
cranking out canapés from six p.m. to midnight. Yes, all

this was impressive, but I never left my kitchen. My hair never left a bun. And no one remembered anything other than my grandmother's favorite things: cheese logs, onion dip, mail-order ham, and Nutter Butter snowmen. That's what guests don't want to admit that they want to eat.

Nowadays, I pick through flea markets and eBay to find recipes for delicacies just like them in vintage cookbooks.

"Vintage" is Southern Lady Code for *dog-eared, with ballpoint notes in the margins*. If the title includes Junior League or Women's Club or the name of a small town; if the pages offer no pictures *or* seemingly impossible photos of shrimp in a bread loaf or Spam shaped like a circus train; if some of the recipes read "Mrs. So-and-So's Husband's Favorite Such-n-Such," I know I've got myself a winner. Cheese logs are found in the appetizer section, listed alphabetically between Bar-B-Q Cups and Coke Salad.

For a Hawaiian Cheese Log: Drain canned crushed pineapple, then wring it out in a dish towel. Add chopped bell pepper. Add Worcestershire sauce. Yes, you need that much cream cheese. Yes, you should wait for it to reach room temperature because there's no worse way to give yourself tennis elbow. Mix. Shape mixture into a log. Or a candy cane. Or a reindeer's head. Go nuts. Cover in nuts. Wrap in wax paper. Refrigerate for up to two weeks. The magic words are: Make ahead. The flavors will marry. Orgy is more like it. Yes, it sounds disgusting and doesn't look much better.

"Is this homemade?" a guest will ask.

What she means is: *That looks like a chew toy*.

Slather some on a Ritz cracker and choo-choo it toward her mouth. One bite and she's speaking in a Southern accent. *Oh. My. Gawd*. One bite and she's experiencing both salty and sweet; crunchy and soft; tropical and suburban.

"You made this!" she'll say.

What she means is: *You're a miracle worker*.

Grin as she peer-pressures other guests to try the log. Everybody's doing it! And why not? It's fun to do something you're not so sure you should do. It gives you a rush. Like streaking through a Best Buy.

Onion dip is not as exhilarating, but stir one packet into a sixteen-ounce tub of sour cream and you've got yourself a crowd pleaser. No, you can't substitute low-fat sour cream because it most certainly does not taste the same. No, store-bought dip-in-a-jar doesn't taste the same either. One tastes like a dirty dollar bill and the other tastes like a waste of money. Full-fat is the only way to go. It's a Christmas party, not a funeral reception. Fine, fine, you can also serve it at a funeral reception. But either way, serve with Ruffles because nobody wants to dip celery sticks.

The only thing simpler is mail-order ham. Mail-order exists because it saves time, energy, and tastes exactly like the ham you ordered last year. Mine comes from South Texas. It's hickory-smoked and spiral-sliced. It's six to seven pounds. It's fuchsia-pink and it glistens. It's irresistible. A few sheets to the wind, someone will cradle it like a baby.

Speaking of babies, some hostesses think Nutter Butter snowmen are only for kids' parties. They are not. First of all: Peanut allergies. One face full of hives and your party is over. And, honestly, the work put into these showstoppers makes them too good for kids.

What you do is: Submerge a Nutter Butter in white chocolate. Add mini chocolate chips for coal eyes, orange gel icing for a carrot nose, mini M&M's for coat buttons, and pretzel sticks for arms. Cool on wax paper. Repeat until your apron is more splattered than a Jackson Pollock. Trust me, there will be more Nutter Butter snowmen Instagrams than selfies.

See, I've learned that no matter where they're from or how old they are, people like food that's fun. They like to be daring. They like to eat art. And they like to party like it's 1979 at holiday time.

"Give your guests what they want," Grandmother said.

That's Southern Lady Code for: *There's nothing less fun than caviar on toast points.*

HOW TO BE THE

BEST GUEST

Everyone appreciates a hostess with the mostest, but a hostess with the mostest appreciates the Best Guest.

The Best Guest arrives on time and, from the moment she walks through the front door, spews compliments like a sprinkler.

She says, "Oh my word, look at the dining room table! That centerpiece looks like something out of Barbra Streisand's wet dream! Did you bedazzle those two dozen pinecones yourself? You did! Did you take a class for that? You didn't! You could have your own craft show. And, just so you know: your outfit is everything."

The Best Guest does not then hand off a bottle of wine like a relay baton because the hostess has already taken great pains to pick wine for the night. Nor, for the same reason, does she push her homemade cookies.

She has already sent flowers that morning. She spends as much as she would spend on a nice supper. Yes, including alcohol and tax.

No, the hostess's party will not look like a botanical garden. It will look like a liquor mart or school bake sale because not everyone behaves like the Best Guest.

The Best Guest eats what she is given. If an hors d'oeuvre is on a toothpick, she does not sniff it suspiciously like baby-laxative-cut cocaine. She sucks that toothpick clean. And then she asks for seconds.

The Best Guest does not question canapés. She gets a cheese log rolling. She brags to latecomers, "That mango chutney cheddar used to be shaped like Donald Trump!"

She brags about the mini quiches: "I've eaten eight and slipped one in my purse."

The Best Guest goes where the hostess directs her. She does not dawdle. With the speed and enthusiasm of a game of musical chairs, she sits where her place card instructs her to sit.

She exclaims to the hostess, "Your handwriting looks like something off of *Downton Abbey*. Did you take a calligraphy course? You didn't! You could make a fortune addressing wedding invitations. Oh my word, that ham looks like it was glazed by angels!"

The Best Guest then makes conversation with the worst guest, who is talking to no one. The worst guest has been invited because he is married to someone or is somebody's boss or does somebody's taxes. Nobody likes the worst guest because he finds eye contact challenging. He eats hunched over the hostess's wedding china as if it's a trough.

The Best Guest asks the socially awkward accountant, "What's the sexiest of tax forms? Yes, I'm talking to you. You must have an opinion. The FBAR Form 114! Please, do go on!"

And then she leans in and hangs on his every word as if he's Brad Pitt talking about how he made love to Geena Davis in *Thelma and Louise*.

After supper, the Best Guest does not challenge the hostess. When the hostess says she doesn't want help clearing the table, the Best Guest doesn't lift a finger. When the hostess asks that everyone move into the living room for games, the Best Guest takes the worst guest by the arm and leads the parade.

The Best Guest picks the worst guest as her charades partner. When she pantomimes talking on a phone for—TV show, three words; *second* word, one syllable—*Better Call Saul,* she isn't a bad sport when the worst guest guesses: "Brain Tumor! Hair extensions! Oh, one syllable. EAR!"

The Best Guest knows when the hostess has had enough. A telltale sign is when game time is over, guests have gotten into the good Scotch, secrets are spilling, and strangers are getting handsy, but the hostess can't stop staring at the worst guest, who is balancing the remains of his cherry pie on his medically diagnosed "shaky leg."

Before the plate hits the carpet, the Best Guest knows it's time to call it a night.

The Best Guest is the first one in and the first one out.

And she is the first to write a thank-you note because the stationery and pen are laid out by her bedside for when she gets home.

WHEN TO WRITE

A THANK-YOU NOTE

D id you write your thank-you notes?" is a Southern lady's "Good morning."

Mama said it to me after birthdays, Christmases, and countless other occasions when someone gave me a gift or a gift of their time. Now I say it to myself. It's like a mantra. Instead of *Om,* I wake up and think, *Did you write your thank-you notes?* If the answer is no, the writing of the note is my meditation.

I don't write thank-you notes every day, but I do write them for dinner parties or a special night out with a friend. When it comes to marriage, they should amend the bride's vows. Do you promise to love, honor, and write the thank-you notes? You do. Do you have to write a thank-you note to your husband for picking a squirrel corpse out of the roof gutter? You don't.

But it would be nice.

There's nothing nicer than unexpected appreciation. Hallmark doesn't make a card for everything, so sometimes we make a judgment call. No, I don't mean texting. My motto is: if you're grateful, get a pen.

When I became an aunt, I wrote a thank-you note to my godmother for setting an example of how to be a good influence. I wrote a note to a high school friend for saying something kind to me at our twentieth reunion. When I had a tooth crowned, I wrote a note to my dentist (for alleviating my fear of dentists), the hygienist (for holding my hand when the dentist stuck my gums with a needle as long as a Samurai sword), and the receptionist (for politely calling me back to rebook my appointment every time I'd canceled). I wrote a note to a vet for putting our cat down.

But just because I write a lot of notes doesn't mean I *always* write a note. If I can't find something sincere to say about the thought behind an awful gift—and I have thanked people for bad art and canned fruitcakes—I don't bother. Mama didn't raise me to fake it.

For example, I did not write a thank-you note to a boyfriend who gave me Hanes panty hose in his sister's size.

Mama said, "Helen Michelle, that screams *hussy*. Break up."

And I did not write a thank-you note for a box of thank-you cards.

Mama said, "Helen Michelle, giving someone a box of thank-you cards is another way to say *you never say thank you*. It's passive-aggressive. It's like a punch in the face."

Not everyone needs to write thank-yous, though. I'm officially letting these folks off the hook: new moms, the bereaved, and women jilted at the altar. If your breasts are leaking at the Piggly Wiggly, or your daddy's under the dirt, or your bedazzled white dress can't be returned, you don't need to write me a note for a onesie, or a casserole, or a chip-and-dip bowl. And while I'm at it, I'm pardoning teenage boys. Because my idea of hell is being sentenced to read nothing but one-sentence fill-in-the-blank notes written by teenage boys.

But the rest of us should send our thank-you notes. And no, it's never too late.

AN EMILY POST FOR

THE APOCALYPSE

Visiting my parents in Alabama, I sat with my mother over my traditional breakfast of Coke and cinnamon toast and told her a story that my friend had told me about a neighbor who'd blown his own head off, in front of his two young sons, five minutes before his ex-wife was due to pick them up.

Mama said, "Well, that is just rude. Helen Michelle, if you're going to commit suicide, what you do is get into a bathtub fully clothed. That way, when you shoot yourself, your brains will go all over the tiles, and it will be easier to clean up. And since you're not nekkid, it will be less embarrassing for the person who finds you."

All my life, my mother has taught me to be polite in extreme situations. Teaching your children to say "Yes, ma'am" and "No, sir," to chew with their mouths closed, and to pick their noses in private is for amateurs. My mother is an Emily Post for the Apocalypse.

There's etiquette for the insane: "Helen Michelle, that man rocks by the Winn Dixie because he is crazy, but we still wave at crazy people when they wave at us."

Etiquette for phone solicitors: "Helen Michelle, the way you stop someone from calling again is by saying, 'Thank you so much for calling, but I've just murdered my husband and need to finish digging a hole in the backyard. Good-bye."

Etiquette for sons-in-law: "Helen Michelle, when your husband calls me, please have him start with 'Hello, everything is fine, I'm just calling for fill-in-the-blank.' Otherwise, I'll assume he's calling to tell me you've been kidnapped and sold into sex slavery."

Etiquette for hospital visits: "Helen Michelle, after your husband's grandmother has her leg amputated, don't sit on her bed in the flat spot where her leg used to be."

Etiquette for street crime: "Helen Michelle, always carry money for a mugger—three one-dollar bills wrapped up in a five. Keep the cash in your purse flap. This way, when you're mugged, it's easier for everyone involved. You grab the wad of bills, hold it up for the mugger to see, and shout, *This is all I have!* Then throw the money and run, screaming *Officer down!*"

Along with her blue eyes and compulsive need to compliment strangers (I too now can't let a manicure or face full of freckles go unmentioned), I've inherited a gene that tells me how to behave when I walk in on a construction worker masturbating in my apartment.

What you do is freeze. The door to your bedroom is shut and from behind it is coming a lot of heavy breathing. You tell yourself he's watching a Bruce Willis movie on his iPhone on his lunch break. You're tempted to swing open the door and holler, "YIPPEE-KI-YAY, MOTHERFUCKER!" But then you hear what sounds like an otter stuck in a pickle jar.

You do not open the door.

You do not reprimand the construction worker through the closed door.

You do not clear your throat or call out, "I'm home!"

You leave the premises and make a phone call.

This is what a smartphone truly is for. Not for Instagramming pictures of the sky outside your airplane window or asking Siri what year *Die Hard* came out. A smartphone is for calling your interior designer from a street corner to tell him to call his employee and tell him to go. Ladies who confront masturbators in their apartments get murdered.

Manners keep you safe.

Mama says, "Helen Michelle, a lot of women have

trouble saying no and then find themselves in worse situations because they were afraid of being rude. So, if you have trouble saying no, say 'No, thank you.' Let's practice."

"Okay."

Mama says, "Miss, would you like to climb into the back of my unmarked van?"

I say, "No, thank you."

Mama says, "Would you like to have a business meeting in my hotel room?

I say, "No, thank you."

Mama says, "Would you like to drink something out of a gas funnel?"

I say, "No, thank you."

"Sex on a bed of nails? Juggle live monkeys? Stick your head in an alligator's mouth? Stab an icepick between your fingers as fast as you can?"

"Mama!"

"Let me hear it, Helen Michelle."

"No, thank you."

For more than two decades in New York City, Mama's advice has served me well. And more and more I find myself wanting to impart her etiquette to others.

On the subway, I'll ask my husband, "Why is that man rifling through his bag? He shouldn't look the way he does and get onto a subway and rifle through a bag. I'm going to tell him."

"Helen, that's racial profiling."

"It's not racial profiling if he's in camo and night-vision goggles on the 6 train. You don't plant yourself in front of the exit doors and dig in a bag. He looks like a nut job. What's he rooting for? Oh, his Purell."

"Helen, please don't say anything."

"Well, he should know better. Someone should tell him he's frightening us for no reason. Someone should also tell him not to Purell in public. He might as well be rolling deodorant onto his armpits."

Upon hearing this story, my mother adapts like a ninja. In case of a terrorist, she instructs me to carry a makeshift weapon to benefit myself and others, like Granddaddy carried a lighter or Grandmother carried Certs.

"Helen Michelle, what you do is empty a fake lemon juice lemon and fill it with hairspray. Then, when you squeeze it, it's a direct stream to the eyes. It's blinding and completely legal."

Call her crazy or crafty, it's how my mother has taught me to survive. I've been mugged three times and come out unscathed. One time, I forgot the lemon. When the mugger said, "Give me your bags," I said, "No, thank you," and stepped around him like he was a perfume spritzer at Bloomingdale's.

HOW I WATCH

PORNOGRAPHY

LIKE A LADY

I watch pornography like a lady because pornography finds me.

I don't know if pornography finds everyone on Twitter or if it finds me because of my account name: American Housewife. Apparently *American housewife* is a popular search term in the pornography industry. *Apparently* folks like to see an ordinary, everyday housewife have sex with a stranger—be he repairman, yardman, or seven-foot-tall transient of another race or ethnicity with a penis the size of a T-shirt gun lured to the suburbs from a bus depot.

I like to see this for about a minute and twelve seconds, which, on average, is how long a Twitter pornography clip lasts—1:12 is enough for me because it's the surprise that's arousing. Pornography is like seeing someone juggle and thinking, *Huh, I juggle. Is that what I look like juggling?* Or *Huh, I juggle bowling pins, but that lady right there juggles flaming chainsaws. I gotta see that.*

So, I watch. And then, I enjoy myself. "Enjoy myself" is Southern Lady Code for *clitoral stimulation and a nap.*

My husband asks, "I don't have porn in my Twitter stream, does it just show up?"

"No," I say. "It gloms onto me as followers. Like suckerfish on a whale. I have a friend whose last name is Weed, and she gets followers with pot leaves as their avatars."

My husband asks, "So, you actively seek out porn?"

"No," I say, "but I have to find it to report it."

Here's how you spot a Twitter pornographer: The avatar is a picture of an erect penis, a man with his hand on his erect penis, bare breasts, or—if you are wondering what that is a close-up of—vaginal labia. Sometimes there's no avatar, but the bald gray silhouette has a name like a NASA password, hasn't tweeted, and is following the likes of Dubai Call Girls, Indian Sex Videos, Horny Slut, and Massage for Ladies.

Click such a new follower, scroll down one post, and there you have it: Twitter pornography. For example: a video of a woman spread-eagled on her stovetop, gripping her ankles like S.O.S pads.

My husband says, "So you do watch it."

"Yes," I say. "But I don't pay for it or Google it. I'm a

lady. I'm discreet. I put my finger over the camera lens so it won't *see me* watching. Besides, I don't want to get blackmailed."

My husband says, "You're not going to get black-mailed. But is that why you report it? Like, as an insurance policy? Or because you feel guilty?"

"A little of both," I say. "I guess it's like some women run on a treadmill after they were *naughty* and ate a muffin. But mainly I report it because I'm a lady. I didn't *ask* to see it. It's like a freak show. Sure, every once in a while, I want to see a guy hammer nails up his nose, but I don't want a bunch of carnies showing up at my door uninvited and pitching tents inside my house."

"Or force-feeding you muffins," says my husband.

"Exactly," I say.

Twitter writes: "Help us understand the problem with @hornyguy1968. What issue are you reporting?"

My choices are: "I'm not interested in this account," "They are tweeting spam," "It appears their account is hacked," "They're pretending to be me or someone else," "Their Tweets are abusive or hateful," or "Their profile info and/or image include abusive or hateful content."

Since there is no category for pornography, I pick "Tweets are abusive and hateful."

Twitter writes: "How is @hornyguy1968 being abusive or hateful?"

My choices are: "Being disrespectful or offensive,"

"Engaging in targeted harassment," "Directing hate against a race, religion, gender, or orientation," "Threatening violence or physical harm," or "Contemplating suicide or self-harm."

Since there is no category for pornography, I pick "Being disrespectful or offensive."

Twitter writes: "We understand that you may not want to see every Tweet of @hornyguy1968, and we're sorry you saw something on Twitter that offended you." Turns out Twitter speaks Southern Lady Code. "Sorry you saw something that offended you" is Southern Lady Code for: *Get that stick out of your butt, Miss Prissy Pants.*

My choices to disassociate with the pornography are "mute" or "block." Mute makes the pornographer disappear from my view. Block makes us both disappear from each other's.

I block @hornyguy1968.

Out of more than 15,000 followers, I've recently blocked 208 because I am a lady. But I fear that Twitter pornographers are like mice: you kill one in your kitchen, there are thirty more in the walls.

So, I decide to look deeper. I decide to clean my virtual house. And I do it the only way I know how: I look at each of my followers one at a time.

You are who you associate with, and as I scroll through my newest 1,600 followers, for the most part I find married women and moms, sorority girls and gay men, yogis and professional organizers, librarians and booksellers. But mixed in are ninety-eight pornographers. And they ain't all posting American housewife amateur porn.

Here are the video cover images I saw, but did not click: a naked woman penetrated by a penis in her every orifice; a naked woman wearing a hijab with a penis in her anus, being choked; what looked to be a naked twelve-year-old girl holding her breast; and—I can barely stand to write it—a naked woman bent over a bed in front of a donkey.

I feel nauseated and assaulted.

These can't all be willing participants. How are these things in existence, much less on Twitter? How is what I've so easily found not monitored and policed?

So, I try a new tactic to get Twitter's attention: instead of reporting tweets, I report that a *profile image* is abusive or hateful.

Twitter takes notice. "What kind of content does their profile image contain?"

My choices are: "Adult," "graphic," or "hateful."

Since there is no category for pornography, I pick "Adult."

Twitter writes: "If we find that this account is violating the Twitter Rules, we will take action on it."

I don't know the Twitter Rules, but I'm willing to bet gang bangs, rape, pedophilia, and donkey sex are in the Don'ts column.

Twitter writes: "We appreciate your help in improving

everyone's experience on Twitter. Your 7 reports over the past hour will help make this a safer and better place." And then they list the accounts I reported, so I am made to see them again: avatars of penises and accounts named IWank, Bigman, Traphoe, and Dick Sanchez, whose avatar is Anthony Weiner.

My husband asks, "Did Twitter delete their accounts?"

I say, "I don't know. They confirmed that I reported them but don't say what they did about it."

My husband says, "They should. Do you want me to check?"

"No!" I say. "I don't want that in your history."

"So you'll check?"

"No!" I say. "I'm not going to go snooping around accounts I reported. Why is it my job to double-check if Twitter is doing something about it?"

But I do. I email Twitter and set up a phone call with someone in their public relations department. She is polite and patient, but the gist is: Twitter allows porn.

As long as the Twitter account or its tweets are marked as containing sensitive media, or the sensitive media is hidden behind an interstitial, or the sensitive media does not appear in the account's avatar or header, it's cool.

Sensitive media includes *adult content,* which is defined by Twitter as "Any media that is pornographic and/or may be intended to cause sexual arousal." Examples given are "full or partial nudity (including close-ups of genitals, buttocks, or breasts)," "simulating a sexual act," and "intercourse or any sexual act (may involve humans, humanoid animals, cartoons, or anime)."

I have no idea what a humanoid animal is, but like pornography, I guess I'll know it when I see it. And if I see something that violates Twitter Rules, I'm told how to report it. As when I see pornography, I get the sinking feeling I've been doing it wrong. I need to report the tweet. And if I want to stop seeing pornography altogether, I should make my account private or go to my safety settings and uncheck the box that reads, "Display media that may contain sensitive content."

But taking all of these actions won't stop pornography accounts from following me.

I don't know what Twitter gets out of hosting pornography accounts, or what pornography accounts get out of following me. Do they want me to visit their sites and type in my credit card to watch more than 1:12?

I'm not going to do that.

Do they want me to become desensitized to the abuse and objectification of women?

I'm not going to do that.

Do they want me to stop reporting and blocking, and just relax, reset my privacy settings, and accept that pornography is part of my world?

Honestly, I consider it.

But now that I've seen what I've seen, I can't go back to watching what I thought was "okay" pornography. For every video of consensual adults playing Cuisinart in the kitchen, something sinister must exist. Doesn't one form of pornography enable the other? It must. Within the Twitter walls, it's multiplying like mice. In the last twenty-four hours, two out of six of my new followers have been bald gray silhouettes with a penchant for women who unroll their bodies like airplane evacuation slides. Plus, I still have more than thirteen thousand followers left to investigate. And I can tell you, I'm so repulsed and exhausted, I want to quit.

But I'm not going to do that.

This is my house, and I will escort every unwelcome guest out. Because I am a lady. And from now on, I'll use my imagination to enjoy myself.

DUMB BOOBS

Right before my forty-seventh birthday, my gynecologist told me I had to get a follow-up mammogram because I have "dense breasts." "Dense breasts" is the term du jour. This year, every woman I know has dense breasts. Or as I like to call them: dumb boobs. Dumb boobs flunk mammograms. Suddenly all the women in my age bracket have breasts that have thickened like congealed New England clam chowder. If cancer is a green pea in that soup, radiologists can't see that pea. So our dumb boobs have to be retested. Or take harder tests. Dumb boobs.

So back I went to Lenox Hill Radiology, which is run like a Burger King. You're in and you're out in half an hour, and the technicians handle your tits with the ease and nonchalance of someone flipping flame-broiled patties.

And here's my advice about radiology technicians: you want the ones who look like flight attendants who've been pushing a cart since the days of *coffee, tea, or me.* You want older women. *Been there, done that* women. Weathered women. "Weathered" is Southern Lady Code for *someone left the cake out in the rain* (and the cake is that someone).

The last time I had a technician under thirty, she was stunning, with winged eyeliner and red lipstick, but her answer to my hello was: "So you don't get your period?"

I was there for a sonogram because I had a twinge in my belly where my low-rise jeans cut me off. I said, "How old do you think I am?"

She said, "I didn't look at your age on your chart. Are you here for an abdominal or vaginal test?"

I said, "I don't know."

She said, "You've got good insurance, you might as well have both."

I said, "No, thank you."

She left to find out what test she was supposed to administer, then came back and said, "The front desk spoke to your doctor and he says it's abdominal."

"He?" I said. "Who do you think my gynecologist is?"

She looked at my chart and confirmed that my gynecologist's first name is very much a woman's name in the way that Jennifer, Dorinda, and Clarice are most definitely women's first names. She explained, "Oh, I call all doctors *he* because most doctors are men."

"Oh, come on," I said, "be a good little feminist!"

We did not speak for the remainder of my test, which turned out fine. I bought a larger pair of jeans. No more abdominal twinge.

The technician who gives me my follow-up mammogram has a thick gray ponytail and never stops talking. She tells me about her family's history of breast cancer and calls me *honey* and *baby* more than my husband has done in our long life together.

I come from generations of women who do not like to be called honey or baby or anything else that a sexually harassed waitress or secretary or CEO might be called. Mama used to reprimand Papa for calling her "your mother" when he spoke about her to my sister or me.

"My name is Helen!" Mama would shout from another room.

My name is also Helen, and I ask for so much respect that my husband's pet name for me is Mrs. Haris.

But here in this exam room with my top off with this stranger, her terms of endearment are a comfort to me. She sees the likes of me—I'd estimate—four times an hour, eight hours a day. She knows that I'm anxious, whether I want to admit it or not.

If there is a word for the opposite of a hypochondriac, I am that word. I take care of myself, but I don't panic. A headache is just a headache. A cold doesn't need antibiotics. I don't Google symptoms. But I do practice preventative care. "Preventative care" is Southern Lady Code for *sunscreen to ward off skin cancer and a crossword a day to keep Alzheimer's away*. I get annual checkups and, even though I have no maternal family history of breast cancer, since I turned forty, I get mammograms once a year.

But a friend of mine is fifty-eight and never had a mammogram because she's afraid of radiation. My paternal grandaunt, who wore a leopard-print bikini well into her sixties, was so terrified of a mastectomy, she never went to a doctor until cancer ate a hole clean through her skin. One in twenty women are so terrified of finding cancer or something that *looks* like cancer—another technician told me—that they faint with a breast wedged in the machine. Some women bring rosary beads into the exam room. Some cry. It's understandable. The lead aprons and metallic nipple stickers don't put you at ease.

My technician warns me, "Now, I'm gonna get up close and personal."

She comes at me like a linebacker. Or a mom trying to get her kid into a snowsuit.

When it comes to mammograms, you have to give in and give yourself over to the technician. Don't fight her. Go limp like one of those inflatable car dealership wiggly men. Hold your arms up and let her jiggle your breast into place.

I, personally, have tits made for mammograms. They are 36 DD naturals, buoyant and round. Haven't had a mammogram? Picture putting a water balloon between two coffee table books made out of taxicab partitions and flattening that balloon until right before it bursts.

That's how it goes if you have my breasts: Baby Bear in the Goldilocks story of breasts, breasts that are *just right*. But if your breasts are too big, they have to be squashed one section at a time; and if your breast are too small, they have to be wrenched from your torso in a torture akin to what we on the playground used to call Indian burns.

There is a new machine they use to test your dumb boobs, I kid you not, called the Genius. It was invented— I suspect—at the same time as "dense breasts." The Genius takes 3-D pictures and Sheryl Crow is the spokesperson; but for my follow-up, I'm having a regular no-brand-name mammogram with a smaller squeezer. How small? Instead of coffee table books, picture that 1980s TV talking tub of Parkay.

Breast cancer!

Par-kaaaaay!

The technician says, "Now THIS is gonna hurt."

I ask, "Why would you tell me that?"

She says, "What, you want me to lie to you and tell you it's gonna be like lemonade?"

I say, "I most certainly do."

She loads and locks me. It hurts so much I curse like a fourth-grade boy on a field trip. There's maybe a foot between me and whatever button she presses to take the image of my breast, but bless her, she rushes to it. I hear a series of clicks. Even if I wanted to, I can't turn to see what she's doing behind me.

She says, "Don't breathe, don't breathe."

If I breathe, I'll blur the picture. If I blur the picture, she'll have to take another picture. Another picture means more time in the vise.

I hold my breath. And, while it *is* only for a matter of seconds, it's enough time for me to develop a conspiracy theory: the medical community is making money hand over fist off our fear of double mastectomies. So many of us are getting called back for follow-up mammograms and ultrasounds (a test in which your breasts are lubed up like Cinnabons and each is worked over like I used to work over a Centipede trackball). Next year, they're gonna want a biopsy. I'm not gonna want to do it. I wanna go home.

My technician releases me.

As I put on my paper robe, she invites me to come around her protective screen to look at the inside of my breast. There are white specks behind the nipple.

She says, "See that? That's calcification. We don't know what causes it, but it's nothing. It's like soap scum. I'll show this to the doctor and send you on your way."

I hug her and thank her for being so nice to me and my dumb boobs.

And no, radiology technicians are not supposed to tell you about their findings or lack of findings, but here's where getting a weathered technician comes into play. In my experience, older women have been empathetic because they've all found themselves in my exact literal position: getting called back for more tests when we're as cancerous as Irish Spring.

YOUNG LADIES,

LISTEN TO ME

If you don't know what to do with the rest of your life, make your bed. If you're going to be a couch potato, at least fluff the pillows. If you can't afford pearls, red nail polish is your best accessory. If you don't have time to do your nails, smile and stand up straight.

Keep calm and check your carry-on bag. Wait patiently and read a book.

Texting a minute before you're scheduled to meet someone to say you'll be there soon is not being on time. Flip-flops are not shoes. Leggings are not pants. Dying your hair gray is not a good idea. And neither are those inner-arm, rib-cage, and finger tattoos.

If your friend tells you a secret about another friend, she has told another friend a secret about you. Just because someone knocks on your front door doesn't mean you have to open it. If you have to keep telling folks you're not sick, you are sick. If a deliveryman packs two forks, you're overeating. If an item is 75 percent off, there's a reason, so don't buy it. If someone asks you a question that's too personal, say, "Once, in college."

Try to live a life worth impersonating by a drag queen. Name your Starbucks self Rihanna. Flash yourself in your mirror. Take as many bikini pool shots as you possibly can because Sarong City is closer than you think.

SEVEN THINGS

I'M DOING INSTEAD

OF A NECK LIFT

Contouring: Contouring means putting brown blush on my neck. And my jawline. Or where my jawline used to be. I take a flat-end brush and draw lines from my earlobes to my chin. Or where my chin used to be. I could also use a brown cream stick that looks like a glue stick. If they come up with a glue stick that glues my ears behind my head, I will buy that.

Anyhoo, I blend. It's very important to blend. Blending the brown lines makes me look natural. "Natural" is Southern Lady Code for *pretty without trying too hard.* To me, in the eighties, Dolly Parton looked natural. Trying too hard would be getting a neck lift.

If I blend well enough, I'll achieve a sort of smoke and mirrors illusion. My neck will look like a tobacco-stained cigarette pouch and my face a shiny clasp if I highlight with shimmer. These days, matte is out and illumination is in. We women are supposed to glow like those *Cocoon* aliens who skinny-dipped with Wilford Brimley. Good news: If you don't know this movie or actor, you don't need to contour.

Camera angling: When posing for a picture, I no longer say, "Cheese." I say, "Higher." I instruct the picture taker to hold the camera like a piñata. If he doesn't understand my instructions, I scream them. "Higher! HIGHER! Hold the camera like a piñata!" If I want to be sophisticated, I'll say, "Hold the camera like a chandelier."

The photographer's hands and arms should be up over his head like a charging chimpanzee's. He should not be able to see the camera lens. He should tip his phone like an auction paddle and click.

My best angle is that taken by a hovering drone. Scroll through my albums and you'll think I've been under NSA surveillance. But don't I look gorgeous? All my face flesh has fallen back to reveal my bone structure. Just look at my cheekbones. And my neck. What neck?

Top-knotting: To top-knot, I spent two years growing my hair past my shoulders so I can now sweep it up onto the top of my head and twirl it into a ball like a ski-mask pompom. My hair ball can't be too tight because then it looks like a bun. Buns are unnerving. People see a bun and fear I'm about to pull a ruler or hypodermic needle out from behind my back. A top knot should be loose but structurally sound, like a bird's nest. People should want to cup it, to see if it fits in their hand. But if it's too big, people will want to smack it like a *Family Feud* buzzer.

The point is, a top knot pulls my face up. Like bootstraps. My face is the boot. A top knot also draws focus away from my neck like a star on the top of a Christmas tree draws attention away from a tree skirt that is disheveled and lumpy from cats. My neck is the skirt. I don't know what the cats are, but I'll make an appointment with the *good* dermatologist and have them checked out.

Mock-turtling: Although it's tempting to imagine myself as an ear of corn shielded only by silk, once I start buying "lightweight" summer turtlenecks, I can never go back. They make turtleneck swimsuits now too, you know. Lands' End puts bikini bottoms and matching waterproof turtlenecks on catalog models whose necks are as firm and as long as Greek Revival columns. The swim tops aren't marketed as neck girdles; they're sold as sun protection or "rash guards." But turtleneck swim-tops are rash guards the way Colgate travel-size vibrators are "electric toothbrushes."

So until they come up with a turtleneck that doesn't grip my throat like a compression sock, I'll sink into a mock turtleneck like a bubble bath. A mock turtleneck is light and luxurious. Sometimes, I clutch the cashmere collar and bring it up over my nose so I can peep out of my sweater like a kitten over the lip of a teacup. Is there anything more adorable? I don't think so.

Bread-loafing: As an alternative, I'm embracing the fact that my face and neck are beginning to resemble a slice of bread. As soon as I wake up, I look in a mirror and glop on positive affirmations like skin-care cream (or, since I'm bread-loafing, like butter): "Hey there, hot stuff, you *want* your face and neck to look like a slice of bread. Everybody loves bread. People love bread so much, they try and abstain from it. But bread is the great seductress. You, madam, are the Kate Beckinsale of baked goods. Everybody wants you at every hour of every day. Hubba hubba! Those aren't double chins, they are more smiles."

Getting handsy: Forget about my neck, I'll focus on my hands. How often do I see my face anyway? I see my hands a heck of a lot more: reading, scrolling, loading the dishwasher, pulling an arrow out of an intruder—what have you—there are my hands.

Some say the eyes are the windows to the soul, but I say the hands are the tollbooths to beauty. I can Lipo (suck), Thermi (burn), or Kybella (acid-wash) my neck fat away, but there's no plastic surgery for the backs of my hands.

So I moisturize, I sunscreen, I have age spots scraped

off like barnacles. And I don't wear fingerless leather gloves because fingerless leather gloves age you more than using your smartphone light to read a menu.

Antiquing: Screw all this, from here on out I'll consider myself an antique lamp. I am worth something and polished. I may be fragile, but I've survived. I am a conversation starter. And I will never be too old to light up a room.

SERIOUS WOMEN

The *New York Post* nicknamed the twenty-two-year-old woman on trial "Womb Raider."

She'd told everyone she was pregnant. Then she connected on Facebook with a former classmate who truly was nine months pregnant. She lured the victim to her apartment, then took a common kitchen paring knife and slit her throat, stabbed her fifty times in the face, chest, and hands, and then cut open her abdomen. She opened that flap of skin, removed the victim's uterus, and turned it inside out on a bathroom floor like she was emptying a stolen Birkin bag. The baby survived and, for the next few hours, the killer claimed the baby as her own.

It's my friend Meredith's job to send "Womb Raider" to prison for life. And I am sitting in the back row of what will be a two-week trial to watch her do it.

Meredith is private about her work as a Bronx assistant district attorney. She says, "I don't want to ruin anyone's dinner."

On the first day, she wears a skirt suit and leather kitten heels so shiny they look like they're straight out of the box. She is petite and at one point will present evidence—a suitcase with the victim's blood in it—that is nearly as big as she is. She will carry it in her arms like a gigantic teddy bear.

I want to clap and shout, "You go, girl!" or "Yasss, queen!" But I'm pretty sure that's inappropriate. I'm struggling with how to behave because murder trials weren't in my etiquette books. In this audience, one of these things is not like the others, and I am that one thing. I don't look like family (African Americans dressed for church) or press (single women dressed for an Adirondack hike). I'm a middle-aged white lady in a blouse and tapered slacks. My purse has a notepad with notes about ghosts and cheese logs, double chins and Burberry coats. I write silly stories for money. When entering the courthouse, my hair clip set off the metal detector. I feel that detector buzzing all over me now: I am the woman who doesn't belong.

This is a serious room with serious women.

The salt-and-pepper pixie-cut judge, who looks like she's permanently had it up to here, looms down from her bench. The court officer enforces the rules—no texting, no talking, no food, no funny faces—like a headmistress with a handgun. Meredith's co-counsel, a new mom, keeps their desk better organized than a Pack 'n Play. The defense attorney paces, a cougar in a cardigan.

The defendant enters with her wrists handcuffed behind her back. The court officer unlocks her, sits her down, and then takes a seat directly behind her. No one in the audience is here for the defendant. The victim's mother—a pastor's wife—sits with her husband and two adult daughters. Steady and ever present, she is the epitome of composure. God is her jury. I will never hear her speak.

In my notepad, I write to myself: You think you're tough, but you are not tough.

Meredith is tough.

I met Meredith more than ten years ago in a card game. She is the kind of woman whose resting face is a poker face. Nothing rattles her. The woman is calm. And she's not afraid to bet. Throughout the trial, the defense attorney will put her legal pad on Meredith's table, object to her choice of words, and ask the judge to ask her to speak up. When I tell Meredith I'm infuriated that this woman is trying to get under her skin, Meredith tells me she hadn't even noticed.

She shrugs. She says, "I'm missing that gene."

Which explains why she's so intimidating at a poker table. No matter what her cards, she makes it look like she always has the best hand. I can't count the number of times I've folded to her.

Meredith gives her opening statements and lays out the facts. The charges are murder and kidnapping.

The defense attorney goes next.

This woman slinks like a cat who can predict death in a nursing home. I half expect her to rub her side against the jury box to mark it with her scent.

"Oh, she killed her," she says. "She admits that she killed her." But the defense attorney says the kidnapping charge is bogus. And the burden of proof for murder (intent) instead of manslaughter (she snapped) is on the prosecutor (my friend, Meredith).

This is a case about motherhood, madness, and murder. None of which I understand. I don't have kids. And I don't get it: I've never wanted a baby badly enough to do what this young woman did.

The first person to arrive at the crime scene was the defendant's boyfriend. He walked into her apartment and found her sitting by a dead woman with a baby in her arms. He did not want to be there then, and he does not want to be here now. Under the scrutiny of serious women, he swears to tell the truth, the whole truth, and nothing but the truth in a T-shirt that reads MAKE IT RAIN. He glares at his ex-girlfriend and spills out of the witness box like an angry beanbag chair.

The defense attorney tries to discredit his testimony by presenting him as a predator who's been with the defendant since she was fourteen and he was twenty-one. He beat her, he choked her, he sat on her. He denies all of this, but admits that he cheated.

The defense attorney asks him how many women he saw while he was seeing the defendant.

He says, "Too many."

She asks him why one of these women and his very own mother have orders of protection against him.

He says, "Misunderstandings."

She asks him how often he had sex with the defendant.

He says, "Once in a blue."

When I relay all this to my friend Erica, she asks me, "How could he believe he got her pregnant? How could he believe it was their baby? How could he believe she'd been pregnant if she wasn't getting bigger?"

I say, "Every woman carries differently. And he's a man."

Erica asks, "What's that Southern Lady Code for?"

I admit, "She's fat and he's dumb."

I speak in code. My motto's always been: if you don't have something nice to say, say something not so nice in a nice way. The women in the courtroom aren't concerned with being nice.

In my notepad, I write: I have no idea what my friend does for a living.

When Meredith calls me at home that evening, I vow to be direct.

I say, "Oooh, y'all had a HAH-STILE witness!"

Meredith puts me on speakerphone so her co-counsel can hear me. She says, "Please repeat what you just said."

I do. HAH-STILE.

I am a New Yorker who has kept her Southern accent. Southern accents are disarming. Meredith laughs, and I'm glad I've made her laugh because I don't think she's laughed under the weight of this case for a while.

She asks me if I found the boyfriend credible.

I say, "Oh, he's a son of bitch, but I believe him. She did it."

I wish I was on her jury, but I'd never be picked to be on her jury because I know the prosecutor (my friend, Meredith) and, besides that, I can't look at autopsy photos.

When the city medical examiner takes the stand, he is as threatening as a cartoon mouse in a three-piece suit and seems to be perfectly fine with that. The man is wee. There's just no better word for him. He is also so Irish that he sounds like the Lucky Charms leprechaun. He lilts like he's talking about pink hearts, green clovers, and yellow moons, but what he's describing is the uterus, umbilical cord, and placenta, which arrived separately from the victim like a battery pack.

He describes the first photo Meredith enters into evidence as the victim's palms—or as the Irishman pronounces them, "the PAMs," like he's talking about the cooking spray. He says, "There are defensive wounds on the PAMs."

These wounds—along with the cuts on her face, neck, and chest—are superficial. "Superficial" is Doctor Code for *didn't damage muscle or hit bone*. The wounds the jury sees next are dramatic. Here's how another witness described what he saw: "She looked like she'd exploded. Everything that was supposed to be inside was out."

The judge says, "We're going to take a short recess."

I've had my eyes in my lap for hours, now I look up.

The jury files out, but Juror #7 does not. She's slumped, motionless, and her skin is a waxy gray. The court officer shakes her by the shoulder and says her name. No response. She shakes her harder and says her name three more times. No response.

"Clear the audience!" says the judge.

We stand in the hallway. Family, press, and baby D.A.s (straight-out-of-law-school newbies who clutch their smartphones like pacifiers) don't intermingle. I stand alone.

Paramedics arrive. We wait for an hour.

Meredith and her co-counsel emerge and are led into a neighboring courtroom. My friend looks distraught. Her face is red and her eyes are raw. Has she been crying? The only time I've seen her cry was at her father's funeral. I want to go to her now, like I went to her then, but I know that's out of bounds.

A reporter nudges me and asks, "Who are you with?"

At last I'm noticed. I don't belong. But I'm staying.

I say, "Special interest."

"Are you here for the defendant? I'm looking for her family."

I turn into Forrest Gump when asked by Lieutenant Dan if he and Bubba are twins. I say, "We are not relation."

The judge calls us back into the courtroom and announces that Juror #7 fainted and has been excused from the jury. She'll be replaced with an alternate. The trial will continue, but we'll adjourn for the day.

That night, Meredith tells me that the juror really shook her up. The woman was completely unresponsive for a minute and thirty seconds. They'd thought she'd had a heart attack from the shock of the autopsy photos and was dead.

The medical examiner went to her aid, roused her, and later whispered to Meredith, "It's the first time in years I've felt for a pulse."

Meredith asks me, "By the way, what did you think of the medical examiner?"

I say, "I want you to seduce him and bring him into our circle of friends."

Meredith and I are part of a close group. She and I play poker with the men and read books for book club with the women. All together, we have supper and see movies. We celebrate promotions and clean bills of health. We've rung in the New Year. And birthdays are big. The best gift Meredith has ever given me was surprising me dressed as a 1950s housewife for a party. Outside the courtroom, she's always in jeans and T-shirts. Like I said, she is serious. But for me, she was silly. We are good friends but during the trial have fallen into a new and more intimate routine. Every night we speak. And I know this is my chance to be serious for her.

The defendant is a good witness. She's been in jail for two years and is on two kinds of medications: an antipsychotic and an antidepressant. She speaks softly. Her nails are filed and her hands are delicate. She wears eyeglasses and lifts them to wipe her tears. Her story is that the victim came to her apartment and verbally attacked her.

The defendant says: "Words are weapons."

The defendant says: "I felt cornered."

She snapped. The knife she grabbed was meant to peel

apples. It's small, so it doesn't reason that she'd wanted to kill her. But she did.

The defendant says: "I felt like a monster."

But then she saved the baby.

The defendant says: "I felt happy."

The defendant says: "I still believe I did something wrong, but I also believe that God forgives."

The judge nudges a tissue box toward her. Maybe she did snap.

In my notepad I write: Could we lose?

But then Meredith cross-examines her. And Meredith is not deterred by her tears or soft lies. She gently but persistently hammers the young woman with questions like she's tapping a picture hook into a wall. Tap, tap, tap. The picture starts to change. Tap, tap, tap. Like a trick of the eye in a haunted house, the defendant's portrait morphs from meek to maniacal.

An audience member, who as far as I know has seen ten minutes out of ten days of trial, gets up, steps over my knees, and says under her breath: "I think I heard enough. THIS IS SOME BULLSHIT!"

On break, I text this to our book club and it becomes our war cry. "This is some bullshit!"

The jury thinks so too. After closing arguments, it takes them less than five hours to find the defendant guilty of all charges. Meredith wins.

A month later, we are back for sentencing.

As usual, I arrive fifteen minutes before the courtroom doors are unlocked to make sure I get a good seat. The media are already here. And now it's not just city paper reporters; the TV people are here. NBC and CBS. They wear pancake makeup, and one woman wears thigh-high boots and a Band-Aid-tight dress in blood red. Court officers pen them in with three barricades. When the doors open, I walk right past.

No one stops me because now I know I belong.

The serious women in the serious room have softened. The judge has dyed her hair chestnut. The defense attorney is tan from a trip to Bermuda. When Meredith speaks on behalf of the family, her voice quivers, but it is clear.

Meredith says, "We have so little we can do or change, but we can offer justice for this horrific and unspeakable act that destroyed so many lives." She says she spoke to the victim's mother about sentencing, and here is what the silent religious woman told her: "The defendant can ask God for forgiveness. And if he forgives her, she can go to heaven. From prison."

Meredith says, "She is more forgiving than me."

Meredith asks the judge for the strongest maximum sentence: twenty-five to life for murder, twenty-five to life for felony murder, and twenty-five years for kidnapping.

The defense attorney asks for sentencing with compassion.

The defendant sobs and says she's sorry.

The judge says to the defendant: "Your young age doesn't matter."

The judge says to the defendant: "Your abuse doesn't matter."

The judge says to the defendant: "These were not impulsive cuts."

The judge says to the defendant: "You *are* a monster."

The judge sentences the defendant so that she will never be free.

As I'm walking out of the courthouse, I am chased down the sidewalk by a reporter who says, "I never found out who you're with."

I say what I said to her before. "Special interest."

She says, "Right, right, but what are you doing, writing a book?"

I keep walking. And I think, if she or any of the reporters had stayed in the courtroom, she would have seen me wait in my seat until everyone except the attorneys had exited; then as Meredith passed, she would have seen me take her hand and say, "Good job."

I was there for Meredith. That's friendship. I'm serious.

THAT KIND OF WOMAN

I am the kind of woman who gay men call Auntie; who passes along compliments and saves news to tell you in person; who gifts the most useless item on a wedding registry and sings "Happy Birthday" into your voice mail; who looks like she's photobombing her own photos; who does not have children, but says, "Mama like!"

I am the kind of woman who brings plants into her home and then—with only the best intentions—murders those plants; who empties her dryer lint trap and finds three pennies and a googly eye; who has a lazy Susan for sprinkles and keeps Coke cans in her vegetable crisper; who writes something on her to-do list after she's done it.

I am the kind of woman who spends more money on a

bottle of shampoo than a bottle of wine; who adds three capfuls when the instructions read one; who writes self-affirmations in shower steam; who blow-dries her hair an inch from a wall instead of untangling the cord; who looks at a sunscreen display like other women look at a Tiffany's window—and then applies that sunscreen like a meringue pie to the face.

I am the kind of woman who enjoys the mystery of a manila envelope; who has bouquets of pens instead of flowers and never runs out of stamps; who uses a piggy bank and index cards; who is polite to wrong numbers and flips through a Vermont Country Store catalog like it's from Sotheby's; who buys diaries but doesn't write in those diaries.

I am the kind of woman who giggles when she writes the word *erect* on a crossword; who listens to the radio and listens for the mail; who watches the National Spelling Bee and enjoys sitcom plots about bowling; who likes reruns about four ladies talking on a couch, followed by reruns of four *older* ladies talking on a couch; who still misses *Oprah* at four p.m.

I am the kind of woman who walks through TSA like a bride; who strangers warn not to go into certain neighborhoods; who points out subway rats to children; who buys postcards and sends them when she gets back from vacation.

I am the kind of woman who hangs her head out a window to see what the heck is going on out there; who will give you a look instead of giving the person who is annoying her a look; who is more interesting because of what she *doesn't* do; who does not appreciate being told what kind of woman she is.

· ACKNOWLEDGMENTS ·

Mama said: "Helen Michelle, I've always told you: if you worry about what your mama will think, you'll never be a writer."

She also said: "If you ever want to write about a dead body, I'll drive you to a funeral home, crawl inside an open casket, and hold my breath."

Thank you to Mama and Papa, who will do anything to support me.

Thank you to my writing wives, Ann and Hannah, who pushed me to share secrets that they already knew.

Thank you to my friends, the cast of characters in this book, who inspired me and approved the use of their real names: Bernard, Carmine, Martin, Jason, Carolyn, Terri, Patti, Megan, Elizabeth, Stefan, Katy Belle, Vicki, Laura, Laurie, Ellen, Liz, Karen, Nicho, Erica, and Meredith. And a special thanks to Dani, who texted: "My life is yours to write."

Thank you to my friends and family who don't appear in these pages but are a constant presence in my life. Classic Trashy Book Clubbers: Michelle, Lori, and Kay. Bridge Ladies: Jean and Val. The Virtual Porch: J.T., Ariel, Laura, Paige, and Amy. The Game Night Group: Jeremy, Jon, Kevin, Scott, and Tal. Southern Lady Kathleen and Gentleman Bryant. Heather from PCB18, Camille from Puzzle Posse, Koula from Chanel, Doug from Team Tito, and Ellis from Team Lawrence.

Thank you to those who encouraged me to write true stories. About tidying: Emmy and Susanna from Spine Out, Kate from Vintage/Anchor, Dan from *The New York Times,* and Courtney, my mentor. About partying: Shaun from *EatingWell.* About guesting: Elizabeth, formerly of Simon & Schuster UK, and Neil, from *Financial Times.* About being happily married: Alyssa from *Paper Darts.* And about being thankful: Amanda from *Garden & Gun.* I'm especially thankful for her editorial note: "Just let it rip."

Thank you to Bill, Suzanne, and the entire Doubleday and Vintage/Anchor teams and sales force who make a publishing house a home. To Jenny, my stellar editor who has a unique way of enforcing a deadline. To John, who makes my books beautiful. To Julianna, who makes me sound good. To Nora, who catches my mistakes (like when I misspell two of my favorite things: *Pet Sematary* and Froot Loops). To Victoria, a superstar who's now a shooting star. To Zakiya, who holds down the fort. To *Judy! Judy! Judy!,* who puts me in the best light and my work in the best hands. And to Todd, who sends me out into the world but keeps me grounded. You are the Charlene to my Julia. MWAH!

Thank you to my friend, champion, and agent Brettne, who speaks fluent Southern Lady Code. I'm proud to be part of The Book Group, which is entirely woman run.

Thank you to the New York Society Library, where I wrote most of this book in the stacks. And thank you to the librarians who greeted me every day with: "Good morning, Mrs. Haris!"

And last but certainly not least: thank you to Mr. Haris—my husband, Lex—who reads me David Sedaris in bed. You are my Hugh. My every essay is a love letter, and I'm in love with you.